OSPREY MASTERCLASS

Small-Scale Armour Modelling

Alex Clark
Series editor Marcus Cowper

First published in 2011 by Osprey Publishing
Midland House, West Way, Botley, Oxford OX2 0PH, UK
44-02 23rd St, Suite 219, Long Island City, NY 11101, USA
E-mail: info@ospreypublishing.com

OSPREY PUBLISHING IS PART OF THE OSPREY GROUP

Print ISBN: 978 1 84908 414 7
PDF e-book ISBN 978 1 84908 415 4
EPUB e-book ISBN 978 1 84908 876 3

Editorial by Ilios Publishing Ltd, Oxford, UK
(www.iliospublishing.com)
Page layout by Myriam Bell Design, France
Index by Sandra Shotter
Originated by Blenheim Colour, UK
Printed in China through Worldprint Ltd.

11 12 13 14 15   10 9 8 7 6 5 4 3 2 1

A CIP catalogue record for this book is available from the
British Library.

The Woodland Trust
Osprey Publishing are supporting the Woodland Trust, the
UK's leading woodland conservation charity, by funding the
dedication of trees.

www.ospreypublishing.com

Acknowledgements
I'd like to thank my wife Jeaninne for her support
throughout the time I worked on this book. Also my
two young sons, Joshua and Jude, who provided
much needed occasional breaks from writing it.
These usually involved putting me to shame on
video games such as Mario Kart Wii. A big thank you
goes to another small-scale addict, Bob Grimster, for
his advice and allowing me to bounce ideas off him.
I'd like to also thank Jorge Alvear for his encouraging
words and support. Finally I'd like to thank Paul
Alderton and all the other guys at my local club. I've
been conspicuous by my absence at club meetings
over the last year, but I plan to rectify that soon.

CONTENTS

INTRODUCTION

I have written this book as a record of my thoughts, experiences and approach to modelling small-scale military vehicles. My preferred scale is 1/72nd but the techniques I describe for both construction and painting are all equally applicable to the close scale of 1/76th. In fact most of the techniques could be applied to almost any scale including 1/35th, 1/48th and others. Unlike previous books I have written for the Osprey Modelling Series, *Modelling the Panzer IV in 1/72 Scale* and *Modelling the Tiger Tank in 1/72 Scale*, this book mostly focuses on techniques and tips rather than the specifics of vehicle nationality, era or type. I hope that in doing so this will give the broadest appeal to the book and that everyone who reads it will find something useful to take away. The scope of model making is so great that I wouldn't be able to cover every technique I use in enough detail to do them complete justice. The space and format constraints of the book have directed me to take a look at a selection that I feel is the most useful, allowing me to cover them in greater depth. I'm a great believer in the old adage quality over quantity.

RECENT HISTORY

Since the late 1990s many small-scale modellers have talked of a golden age of small-scale modelling. It was around the mid-1990s when one of the major model manufacturers – Revell – started to take a serious interest in 1/72nd-scale military vehicle kits. Prior to this there were certainly many small-scale kits available from the likes of Esci, Hasegawa, Airfix, Fujimi and Matchbox, but the Revell kits pushed the bar higher in terms of the crispness and finesse of the detail. In fact many of these releases had detail comparable to that found on good 1/35th-scale models, and I feel those first Revell kits helped to kick start a revival. Along with this there was an explosion of interest from aftermarket manufacturers with many photo-etched details sets, turned metal barrels and resin accessories hitting the market. Several years later Dragon (aka DML) who were usually known for 1/35th-scale armour kits turned their attention to 1/72nd scale and have since released many excellent models. Some of them, such as the early Tiger I and early Panzer IV variants, included a phenomenal level of detail equivalent to the very best larger-scale kits. Trumpeter of China joined in not long after and there are now other manufacturers producing injection-moulded and resin model kits in this scale – certainly many more than ten or 20 years ago.

A BIT ABOUT ME

I started modelling as a young boy when my parents bought me an Airfix Boeing 747 kit as a Christmas present in 1981. From then on I was hooked and would save my pocket money to buy all types of models – ships, cars, aircraft and other subjects, all in a variety of scales. Gradually I found myself focusing more and more on small-scale armour models, mostly fuelled by the large Esci range in 1/72nd scale and the Matchbox kits in 1/76th. My main interests at the time were centred on World War II vehicles, largely due to the abundance of these subjects compared to those from the modern era. Then at some point in the late 1980s Hasegawa and Esci released a few modern subjects. This sparked an ongoing interest in modern armour. In particular I became fascinated with post-war Russian vehicles such as the T-64, T-72 and the elusive (at the time) T-80. Frustratingly I was not aware of any models of these back then and they were subjects

I could only dream about. Up until I started university I was still avidly building models but then took a complete break for several years as other interests took over. One day after finishing university I was visiting my parents and for a bit of nostalgia decided to stop by the model shop I used to frequent when younger. To my surprise I found a 1/72nd-scale Russian T-80B tank from Matchbox and immediately bought it. I dug out all my old modelling tools and realized then that the modelling bug had bitten again! I would say my current period of serious modelling really started with that kit.

MY MODELLING PHILOSOPHY

I imagine there are many different reasons why modellers enjoy building models. Model construction has a strong technical element to it whilst painting, finishing and presentation allow for artistic expression and creativity. The creative aspect is further enhanced with the opportunity to build vignettes and dioramas. The choice of subject can provide an outlet for historical and research interests. The strength of model making is that it allows complete freedom to focus on these quite different areas to varying degrees. For me, the construction side fits well with my technical/scientific background

and the painting and finishing side provides me with the opportunity to exercise my artistic interests. I strive for historical accuracy as much as possible too but as the historical side isn't as much of a personal interest I tend not to build many dioramas or vignettes.

The phrase 'you are your own worst critic' is as applicable to modelling as anything else and I find myself constantly trying to improve. Many years back I became frustrated that I was spending a lot of time on building and detailing models followed by a much smaller amount of time on the finishing stages. My building skills had a chance to improve much faster than my painting ability and within a short space of time I'd become dissatisfied with my previous painting attempts. This was particularly disappointing

when I'd spent a lot of time on a complex conversion, or adding many corrections and details to a model. At that point I decided I would take on some simpler builds that would give me more chance to focus on improving my painting skills. Since then I've tended to work in cycles of focusing on more complex builds for a while, but then working on a few kits that are more straightforward – not quite out of the box perhaps but ones with little extra work that needs doing to them. It's only really been within the last few years that I feel I've reached a better balance between the two. That's not to say there's no room for improvement in both areas. Far from it and as many other modellers no doubt often think of their own models, the best one is usually their most recent one!

TOOLS AND MATERIALS

Over the years I've gradually built up a good collection of modelling tools and equipment, and those I describe here are relevant to all types of scale modelling, not just small-scale armour. Some specialist tools can be expensive and these include things such as lathes, milling machines and others but so far I've managed without these. They can also take up quite a bit of space, often more than most people without a dedicated workshop or hobby room have and so for both these reasons I won't be covering them in this book. Resin casting materials could be considered advanced or specialist, but beginner casting sets are available at reasonable prices and they don't require much room to use. With these you can make multiple copies of simple homemade parts without the need for expensive casting equipment, and so this is something that I will be looking at in more detail later in the book.

GENERAL CONSTRUCTION AND ASSEMBLY

I use a small, quite basic set of tools for most of my modelling needs, with other tools being used only occasionally or even very rarely. In the sections below I cover most of the tools I currently own and highlight those I find the most useful. In the past I may have been tempted to buy the latest modelling tool in the belief that it would solve all my most important modelling needs. In practice I found this to rarely be borne out. As such I don't believe you need a big modelling budget or a vast array of tools to build high-quality models.

CUTTING AND SAWING

Although there are many hobby and craft knives on the market, I've used a simple surgical scalpel for many years now. The all-metal handle is very hard wearing and the same one has lasted me for 15 years – it quite possibly will last another 15. The blades are extremely sharp and fine, and I've found it to be excellent for small-scale work. There are many sizes of blade available but I almost always use the 10A size.

For sawing I use a very fine razor saw from JLC of the Czech Republic. I've tried a number of different razor saws over the years and this is by far the best. The blade is thin and the teeth are very fine, both of which minimize the amount of material lost when a cut

I use a few tools for cutting. Shown here are a scalpel, razor saw and Tamiya side cutters and a small pair of scissors. To the right are a compass cutter (for creating discs), Olfa panel scriber and micro chisel.

is made. In fact one of the uses toured by the manufacturer is the cutting of aircraft canopies where material loss would be a major problem. Each blade actually has two sets of teeth, fine and extra fine, both of which I use regularly.

When cutting plastic parts from sprues I use the scalpel for small or delicate parts, but for most other items I use a pair of Tamiya side cutters. They enable a close cut to the part leaving almost nothing to clean up in most cases. One thing to avoid is cutting wire or anything harder than plastic as the cutters can easily become damaged. I also use another older and slightly damaged pair for snipping chunks of resin and other tougher parts.

A tool that I don't use often but that can prove very handy is a compass cutter. The sole purpose of this is for cutting varying sized discs from paper, card or plastic sheet and I just use a cheap plastic one I picked up from an art shop.

HOLDING PARTS

Picking up and holding parts, particularly those that are small and delicate, can be tricky. I use tweezers mostly, although for smooth or curved items care must be taken not to apply too much pressure otherwise they can ping out of the tweezers and be lost forever. Attaching a small piece of

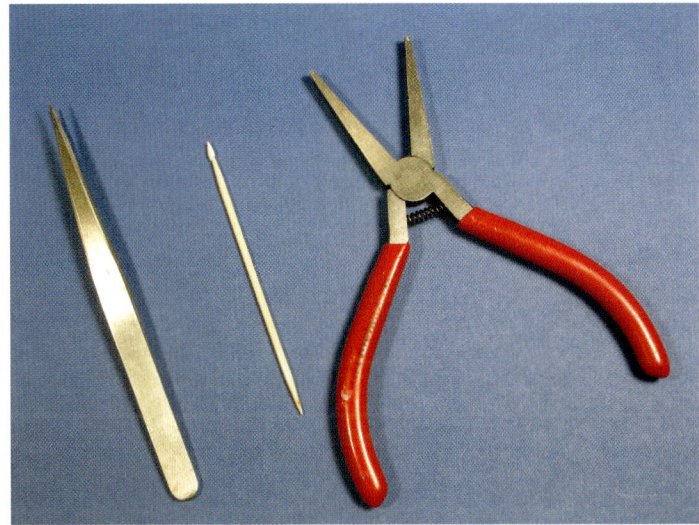

Point-ended tweezers are essential for picking up small parts. For those that are particularly small I use a small blob of Blu-Tack reusable putty on the end of a cocktail stick. Flat-nosed pliers have many uses but are particularly good for holding and bending small photo-etched parts.

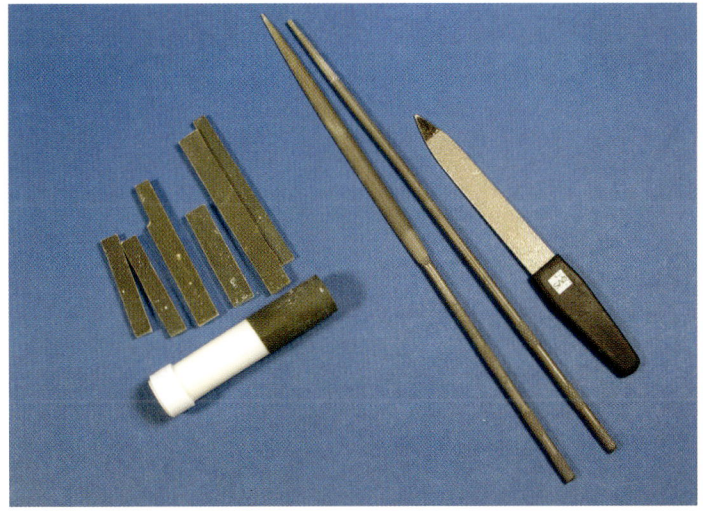

I use a selection of grades of wet and dry paper for sanding parts. I also use these to make my own sanding sticks. Metal needle files come in a variety of cross sections and are longer lasting than sanding sticks. Fine-grade metal nail files are a readily available item, something I gravitate towards when I find myself in a cosmetics shop with my wife!

Blu-Tack reusable household putty to the end of the tweezers will help avoid this by providing some temporary adhesion. Blu-Tack is also useful when attached to the end of a cocktail stick. It's strong enough to pick a part up but not so strong as to keep hold of the part when you want it to let go. I should add here that Blu-Tack is the most well-known type but there are other colours available too and I often use the white variety. In all cases I'll just refer to it as Blu-Tack, whatever the colour. For the very smallest items a cocktail stick with the end dampened can provide enough temporary adhesion in most cases. This is a technique I use when attaching tiny rivets and I'll revisit this later in the book. A good quality pair of flat-nosed pliers is useful for holding photo-etched parts when cleaning them up or folding them.

SANDING AND CLEANING UP

For sanding and cleaning up I use a selection of fine-grade wet and dry paper sheets. Grades 400 and 600 are the two I make the most use of, with the coarser grades only making an appearance occasionally.

A metal rule is a cheap, but essential tool for scratch-building. For small-scale models a short one, about 6in. long, is good enough but occasionally I need to use a larger, foot-long version. A simple set of mechanical callipers is also useful. A try-square is also invaluable.

Before starting each modelling project I make a selection of homemade sanding sticks from plastic strip sections superglued to these sheets. They are then trimmed to size, providing an easy and cheap way to make a lot of them in many different sizes.

Metal needle files are another useful addition to the toolbox and come in an assortment of cross-sections. I make the most use of the tapered circular type, as these are perfect for widening small holes. They are also of use when creating curved corners, for example when opening up hatch holes. Metal nail files are similar and can be found in most cosmetic shops. They're a bit wider and flatter than needle files and I tend to have a couple of these in my tool selection.

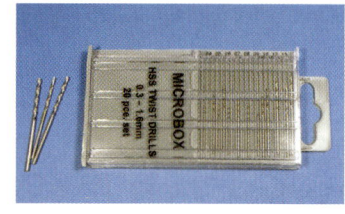

A set of micro drill bits is essential for scratch-building and converting. They're also useful for simple detail improvements such as opening up gun barrels or drilling location holes for wire grab handles.

DRILLING HOLES

Another tool (or more accurately set of tools) I tend to use often is the micro drill bit set. The most common uses are for opening up gun barrels, from machine-gun size to main gun bores, and for creating location holes for replacement grab handles. They have other uses too, especially when scratch-building,

and a set ranging from 0.3mm to 1.6mm provides sizes for most occasions. Other sizes can be bought individually too and I have a few that are larger than any of those in the set.

MEASUREMENT AND ALIGNMENT

Steel rules are one of the most basic tools needed for scratch-building and conversion projects. A 6in. rule is the size I use most with a 12in. version for the odd occasion. Another item that I tend to use often is an engineer's try-square. I have a couple of all steel ones and they are composed of two parts, a stock and a blade. The stock is a thick slab of precision-machined steel and the blade (despite its name) isn't actually sharp but is a thinner plate of steel set at a right angle to the stock. It makes cutting

perfectly rectangular pieces of plastic very easy and is handy for ensuring parts align at 90 degrees.

GLUES AND ADHESIVES

Glues of course are one of the most fundamental craft and modelling supplies and this is reflected in the wide choice that is available. I still use good old polystyrene cement for most plastic-to-plastic bonds although not for the smallest parts. For other materials my first choice is superglue gel as this bonds most things very strongly and has gap-filling properties. It also allows for a small amount of repositioning time and this is something lacking with standard superglue. A strong glue for almost any material is Evo Stick Serious Glue. I'm a big fan of this as it's close to superglue in strength but allows about three minutes for

repositioning. Two-part epoxy glues are also useful in many of the same situations but the Evo Stick glue saves the hassle of mixing the parts. One big difference between polystyrene glues and epoxy/superglues is that the former melts the plastic to form the bond whereas the others tend not to damage the surfaces being bonded. Because of this it's best to avoid using polystyrene glues on very thin or small plastic parts as it can damage them. For scratch-building superstructures I also steer clear of such glue as it can cause a small degree of shrinkage that ultimately will lead to warping.

PUTTIES AND FILLERS

For filling large gaps between parts I use Milliput two-part epoxy putty. It has a long working time and once set is extremely hard but easy to sand. MagicSculpt is also a two-part epoxy putty and has quite different mechanical properties compared to Milliput. Whilst workable, Milliput can tear easily whereas MagicSculpt has a more elastic nature to it. When rolled into a thin sheet this makes it ideal for representing tarpaulins and fabric. In fact it is popular amongst figure modellers for this very reason.

There are many types of glues available and I make use of several depending on the situation. Some of them, such as superglue gel and plastic cement, have gap-filling properties which can save on filling small gaps later on.

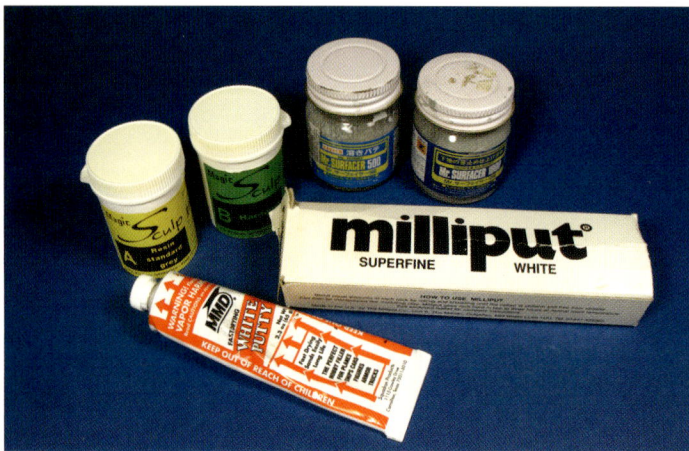

For filling gaps I use Milliput two-part epoxy putty. MagicSculpt is another two-part putty with quite different characteristics. These make it great for simulating folds and creases in cloth and tarpaulins. Mr Surfacer is a type of liquid putty aimed at filling very small scratches. It's also useful for other things, such as recreating surface texture on cast turrets.

For filling small gaps and scratches the Mr Surfacer range of liquid putty is ideal. This comes in several varieties marked with a number: 500, 1000 and 1200. The lower this number the coarser the granule size and thicker the putty. For modelling armour I've only ever used the 500 grade.

STRUCTURAL MATERIALS

For any form of conversion or scratch-building some additional structural materials will be required. My favoured ones are those made of plastic such as plastic sheet (or card), rod, tube and strip. As with injection-moulded plastic kit parts these are easy to cut, sand, glue and paint. Other materials are useful due to their different properties and I have a small selection of thin brass sheet ranging from foil to about the thickness of photo-etched parts. The extra strength of brass compared to plastic is essential in some cases and its properties, such as pliability, are more suitable when scratch-building items such as sheet

metal parts. Metal wire in a range of thicknesses is also very useful. It can be used to replace overly thick grab handles, hoses, tube and loops. Softer metals such as brass and copper are good for making hoses and tubes that require soft curves and bends. Steel wire is stiffer and better for grab handles that may just need a couple of 90-degree bends. In this material they will benefit from being a bit sturdier once on the model. There are some types of steel wire that are quite springy and very difficult to bend. If thin enough these are ideal for making straight aerials, as they are unlikely to bend accidentally.

For detailing, scratch-building and converting kits a selection of different shapes and sizes of plastic items is essential. The Evergreen brand from the US is my personal choice due to the extensive range they provide. The quality of the plastic is also very good and it's easy to cut, sand and glue.

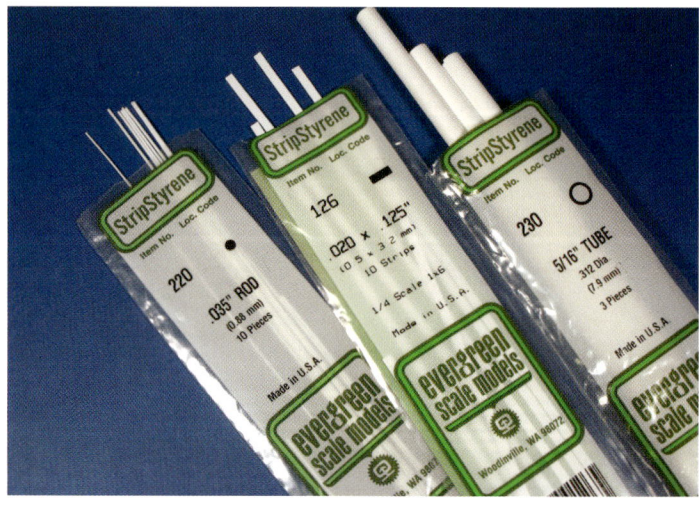

PHOTO-ETCHED BENDING TOOLS

Many years back a number of tools for working with photo-etched parts appeared on the market and since then have become quite popular. These invariably feature a smooth, flat metal plate with another plate that sits directly on top. This upper plate may have a number of differently shaped and sized cutouts. Flat etched metal parts are clamped between the two and can be folded up along the edges of the top plate. I have quite an old version of one of these but I only use it rarely, even though most models I build will involve some degree of etched parts. A simple pair of flat-nosed pliers and a steel rule suffices most of the time, with the specialist tool being useful for long parts such as fenders.

RIVETING TOOLS

A punch and die set is a useful addition to the detailer's toolbox and can generate a number of differently sized small plastic discs for many purposes. For small-scale modelling the smallest size punch is fine for large rivets, but for smaller rivets alternatives need to be found. An excellent tool for these is the Nutter. It's specially designed for making small to very small sized bolt heads, nuts and rivets and I take a closer look at it in a later chapter.

PAINTING AND FINISHING

As with the tools used to build and construct models, the choice of paint brand and finishing materials is a very personal thing. Some modellers can get quite passionate about their choices but in terms of results I've seen many excellent models finished using many different types and brands of paint.

PAINTS

For the majority of my painting I use Humbrol enamels. This is partly down to the fact that they are readily available here in the UK where I live. They have a fairly good range of colours, spray well through an airbrush and once dry are hard wearing (some of the following weathering steps can be quite harsh on the paint underneath). I have tried acrylics but by that time I'd invested quite a bit in building up a collection of enamels and so didn't switch over. I do find that the enamels aren't as good for brush painting and so for smaller details I use acrylics, mostly Vallejo but also some Tamiya and those from the Games Workshop ranges. In particular the lighter colours brush paint much better than enamel equivalents due to the

Left: One of the popular types of photo-etched bending tool. Although these are well made and designed, I don't really use them that much. Almost all the etched parts I use can easily be bent using flat-nosed pliers and a steel rule.

Below: A standard round punch and die set. Hexagonal ones are also available but I don't own one of these. For very small rivets and bolts I use the Nutter. This punches the rivets from a thin, laminated metal foil sheet.

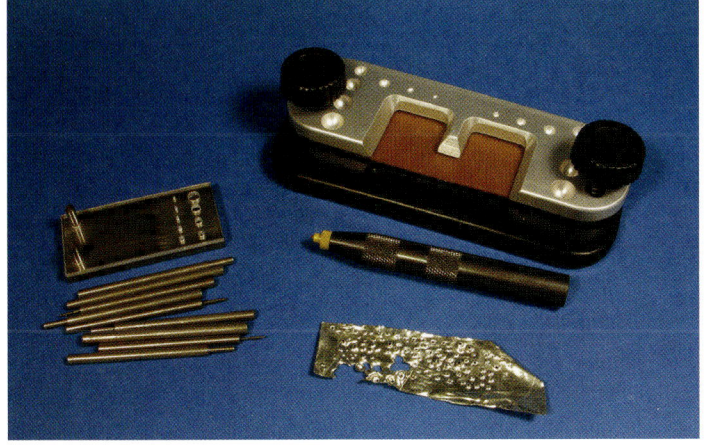

The choice of paints is a very personal thing, with some modellers swearing by acrylics and others preferring enamels. I use enamels for the bulk of my painting but I have a small selection of acrylics and oil paints that come in handy for weathering and detail painting.

more opaque and vibrant nature of the acrylics. There are some cases where I use acrylics as the main colour and I'll return to these later. Oil paints are a favourite of mine for weathering and shading of both vehicles and figures and as they're compatible with enamels I often mix the two together. This helps speed up the rather long drying time of oils but allows additional working time over pure enamel.

WEATHERING POWDERS AND AGENTS

These days there are many weathering and finishing agents available including pre-mixed

washes, filters/glazes and pigment powders. I've used some of these over the years but for the filters and washes I'm happy enough mixing my own. Having said that, I can see that having them pre-mixed is convenient and this will appeal to many modellers. Pigment powders are a ready-ground substitute for pastel chalks that are good for representing dust and other effects. Apart from the convenience of being very finely

ready ground, they have stronger and more vibrant colours than most of the pastels I've used.

PAINTBRUSHES

There's not much to say about paintbrushes apart from it's worth spending a bit more for good-quality ones that won't shed hairs whilst being used. Brushes aimed at modellers seem to be quite expensive, even compared to professional artists' brushes, so I buy most of mine from art shops. For applying washes I use wide flat brushes as these are more suitable for large areas. A medium-sized flat brush is useful for smaller areas and for dry brushing. For detail work and figure painting I use the smallest-sized round brushes. I dilute enamels with the same brand thinners as these are formulated especially with these in mind.

Shown here are some finishing products that are currently available. These generally fall into two types, dry powders and very dilute paint filters or glazes.

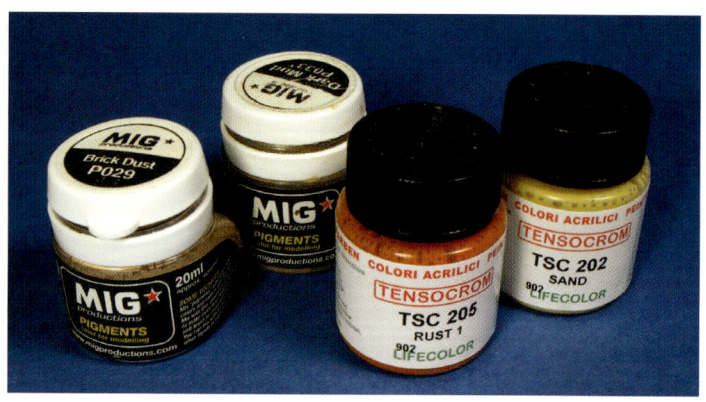

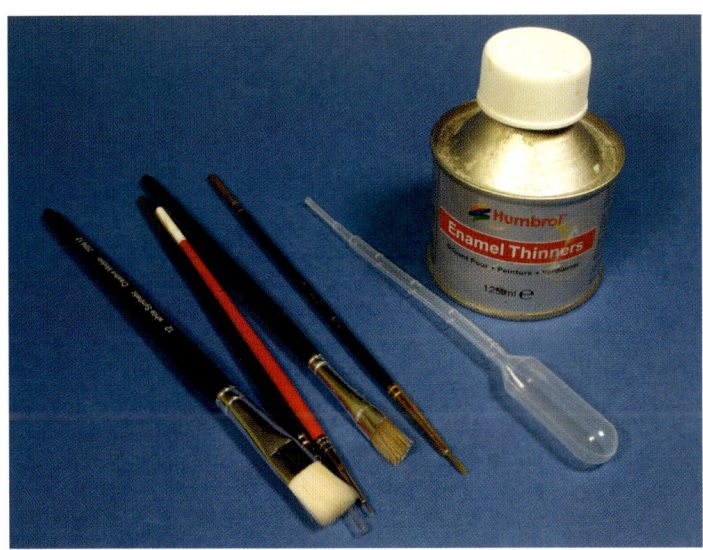

A good selection of brushes is essential. I have some fine pointed brushes for detail work and flat, broader brushes for applying overall washes and dry brushing. When using enamels I wash the brushes in Humbrol thinners, followed by rinsing in warm water. Also shown here is a cheap plastic pipette. I find these indispensible for measuring out paint quantities and thinners.

AIRBRUSHES, COMPRESSORS AND SPRAY CANS

For serious modelling I unreservedly recommend a double-action airbrush. When first starting out I just brush painted my models and after a while progressed on to using spray cans for single all over colours. This improved the finishes I achieved but couldn't be used for sprayed camouflage patterns or to achieve good weathering effects. After this I quickly moved on to an airbrush. Airbrushes come in two main flavours, single-action and double-action. The single-action types are at the cheaper end of the market as the amount of paint sprayed is set just before spraying begins. In contrast a double-action airbrush allows you to vary the amount of paint flow whilst painting. This extra degree of control makes them more expensive but much more versatile in the effects they can achieve. My first true airbrush many years ago was a cheap Humbrol double-action model. Being a budget version it had a plastic rather than metal body and the thinnest line it could spray was thicker than more expensive airbrushes. Still, it served me well in getting to grips using an airbrush and my next one was a higher range Badger 150. I still have this and it's a very reliable tool that works as well as the day I bought it. Currently I use an Iwata Eclipse CS, which is of comparable ability, and I keep the trusty Badger one as a backup.

Along with a good airbrush you'll need a supply of compressed air. If you don't plan on using an airbrush much. cans of compressed air might be a reasonable option. I used these when first starting out but as my demands increased and I wanted to practise more it became worthwhile investing in a compressor. You can get models at the lower end of the price range without all the frills and my first compressor was of this type. It was a bit noisy but did the job of providing a steady stream of air at a constant pressure. After that I moved onto a pricier model that is much quieter and has an integral moisture trap and reservoir. A moisture trap is a necessity really when painting with enamels as any water vapour that gets in the line will adversely affect the paint quality. They can be purchased separately, so it's not vital that one is built into the compressor. A built-in reservoir allows you to build up spare pressure and then use it from the tank silently for a while. Some models will also detect when the reservoir is running low and automatically turn on again. This might not always be a good thing as a modeller at my local club told me. This happened to him with his then new compressor. He almost jumped into the air when it kicked in again after going silent!

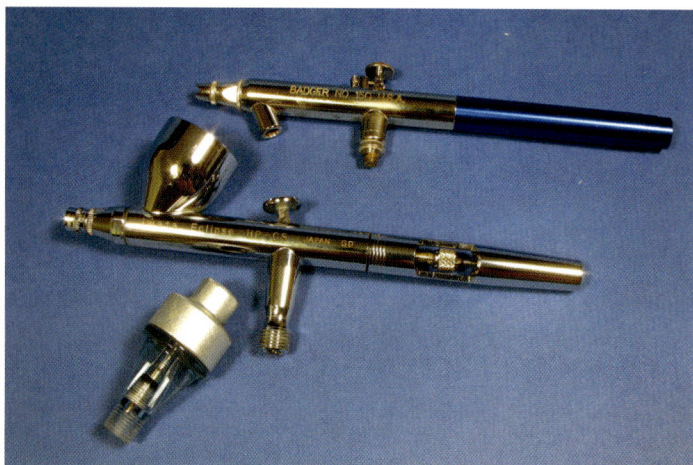

Airbrushes are quite expensive bits of kit but I feel the investment is well worth it. Not only do they give excellent paint finishes but they are perfect for creating a number of weathering effects. I own a Badger 150 and an Iwata Eclipse, both double-action models that are comparable in quality and performance.

For those planning on a lot of spray work, a compressor is much more cost effective in the long term than airbrush gas cans. This compressor has a built-in moisture trap and reservoir for storing compressed air and this allows it to work silently for a time.

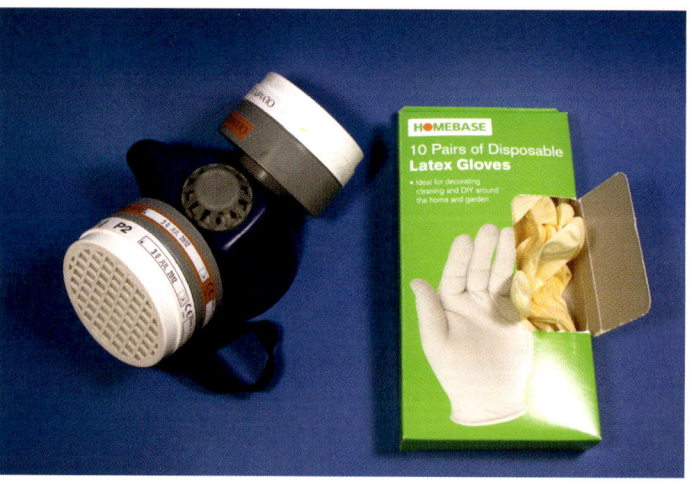

No coverage of modelling tools would be complete without mentioning safety equipment. Thin latex gloves are useful for when airbrushing or working with resin as they allow for precise movement and touch. Adequate ventilation is also essential, particularly when spraying paint. A good-quality respirator will prevent you from inhaling paint fumes. You need to make sure you buy one that has filters for organic solvents. The one shown here has replaceable filters on the sides.

GENERAL CONSTRUCTION TECHNIQUES

There are some fundamental construction techniques that are applicable to any level of modelling, whether straightforward out-of-the-box builds, minor conversions or complete scratch-builds. Rather than spend valuable space discussing these low-level basics I'm going to take a look at some additional tips, tricks and techniques that readers may find useful.

CLEANING UP PARTS

Even the best-moulded modern kits will need some work devoted to cleaning up the parts. By carefully snipping them from the sprue, small burrs left behind can be minimized but are still likely to need some attention. Mould and seam lines will also be present to varying degrees, and for older kits some degree of flash might be visible. Flash can simply be trimmed away with a scalpel whilst seam lines can be gently scraped down. However, some kinds of parts pose additional challenges when cleaning them up. Circular items such as wheels, tyres and gun barrels can be included in this category as it's difficult to maintain the integrity of the curvature whilst sanding and scraping. It can be even more of a chore removing mould seams from main gun barrels due to their length, and in the worst cases the barrel may be a single piece but show some degree of mould shift. This is where two parts of a mould are slightly offset rather than being perfectly aligned. This can have disastrous consequences as to achieve a perfectly round barrel would involve removing too much material, thereby resulting in a barrel that is far too thin. As such I'll always look for turned-metal aftermarket replacements. These barrels are made of either aluminium or brass or sometimes a combination of both. Most makes are reasonably priced and they can provide a number of advantages to kit barrels. They will of course have a perfectly round cross-section and be completely straight. Being made of metal they also have a greater strength than plastic or resin and so won't bend or easily snap. Even a tiny amount of curvature along a barrel length will be quite noticeable by the naked eye. As they don't require any cleaning up there is no danger of ruining the shape either. For barrels with muzzle brakes some of the best replacements have some astounding detail. Most kit muzzle brakes are a little soft on the detail, largely due to the complex nature of the shape and the holes present in it. Many of the Dragon kits use multi-part slide moulds for the barrels and this allows them to be hollowed out. They even have quite good muzzle brake detail in most cases. Still, turned-metal

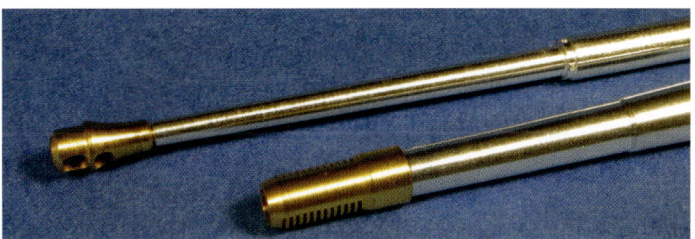

Aftermarket turned-metal barrels can save time on cleaning up the kit parts and often offer superior detail. These sets from Aber feature aluminium barrel sections with very finely detailed brass muzzle brakes. They are some of the best examples available.

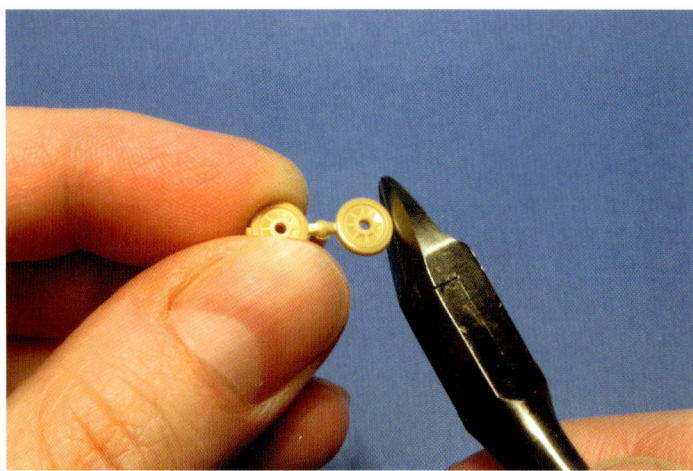

Sprue attachment stubs can be removed by snipping close up to the part with a good quality pair of side cutters.

A short piece of plastic rod that fits tightly into the wheel will allow it to be held firmly within the rotary tool when cleaning it up.

This particular tool is low powered and ideal for small plastic items. Gently holding a fine-grade sanding stick against the part whilst it rotates will slowly remove the seam. Only use a little pressure as it's better to take a bit longer than remove too much material.

Once the seam line has been ground away the excess strands of plastic can be removed from the edges. Giving a very quick and light run through with a piece of wet and dry paper will do this.

Another quick spin against a cheap toothbrush gives the part a final polish.

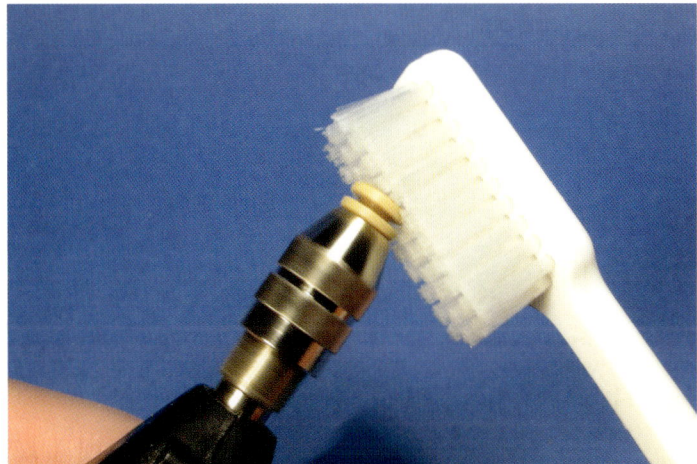

Unlike the wheel in the previous example, this steering wheel has the steering column moulded in place and it can just be dropped straight into the pin-vice. A piece of fine-grade wet and dry paper wrapped around it will remove the seam and also maintain the part's compound curvature. I wouldn't try and clean this part up with a powered tool due to its delicate nature.

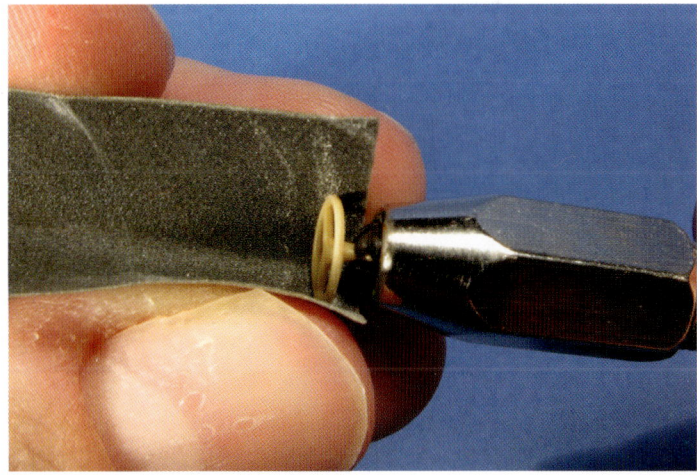

replacements are usually far superior in most respects. A final reason to replace kit barrels is for those cases where the provided one is inaccurately proportioned. Possibly one of the worst barrels I've seen on an injection-moulded kit is that on one of Revell's earlier 1/72nd-scale kits, the StuG IV. The muzzle brake was closer to 1/35th scale and looked grossly out of scale. Of course this can also work the other way and I always check with scale plans if available to ensure I'm not replacing an accurate kit barrel with an inaccurate metal version.

I'm going to look at two simple and similar techniques for cleaning up circular parts, notably wheels. The first involves the use of an electric rotary tool – the kind used to fit drill bits and grinding heads. The best ones have an adjustable power setting which should be set to the lowest one possible. Alternatively, fixed low-power ones are just as suitable. The soft nature of plastic means that it's all too easy to grind away a sizeable portion of the part itself if the setting is too high. A higher power can generate a lot of friction heat that might melt the plastic.

A related technique involves the use of a pin vice to which the part is attached. This is useful for more delicate items or as an alternative for those without access to a powered version.

DEALING WITH EJECTOR-PIN MARKS AND SINK HOLES

Most kits contain parts that have at least a few ejector-pin marks and these are the results of the sprue being removed from the moulds during manufacture. They are usually small, round impressions found on the rear of larger pieces (or in the worst cases on the front obscuring the detail). They can also be either raised or sunk into the part. The raised ones are easier to deal with and just require careful sanding down, perhaps with some initial trimming.

Ejector-pin marks of the depression type need filling. For shallow ones I just use a few applications of Mr Surfacer liquid putty painted on with a small paintbrush. For deeper holes I fill the bulk in with plastic discs. These can either be created with a circular punch and die set or from slices of plastic rod (or stretched sprue) of the correct diameter. After applying a small blob of superglue to the hole, the disc can simply be dropped in place and pushed down. Unless the disc is of the exact thickness it needs to be, you may need to trim a thin layer off the top, or perhaps build it up a little more with some Mr Surfacer. In either case I give it at least a single thin coat of Mr Surfacer at the end anyway to ensure there are no remaining gaps or scratches. Once dry, a light sanding will result in a smooth, blemish-free area.

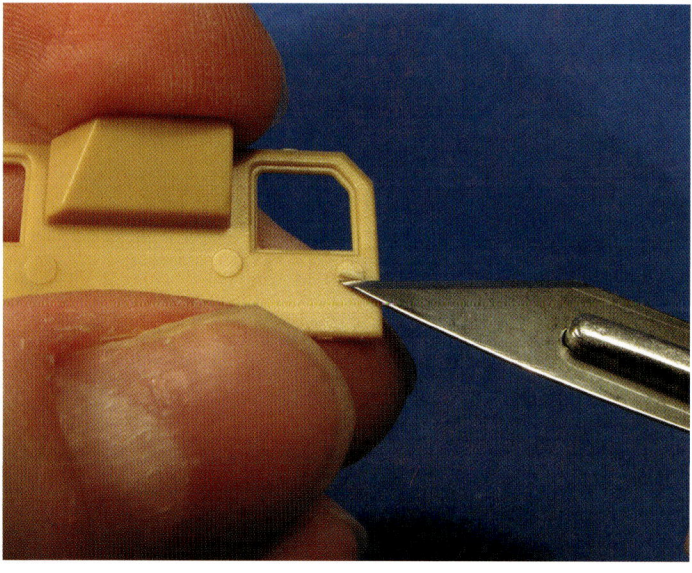

Raised ejector-pin marks are much easier to deal with than the sunken kind. Slice the bulk of them off with a fresh scalpel blade and then gently sand the remaining area flush with the surface.

Unless a sunken ejector-pin mark is very shallow, a plastic disc can be used to fill the bulk of it. The disc should be made using a punch and die set. If you don't own one of these, or don't have one containing the appropriate diameter hole, a slice from some plastic rod or stretched sprue will work equally as well.

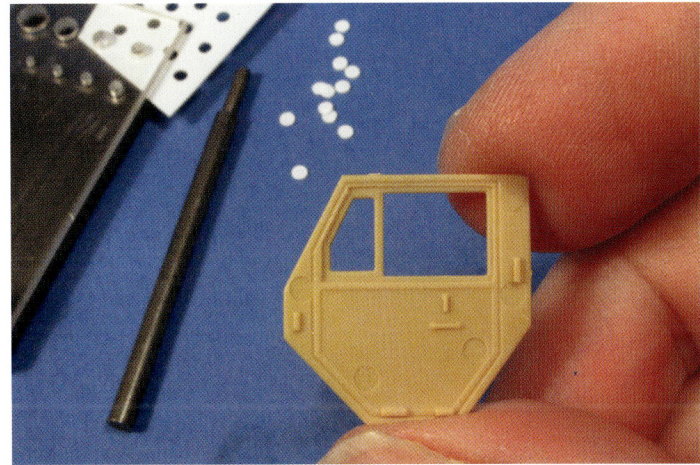

The disc is best glued in with superglue gel and if it sits proud of the surface the excess can be removed with a scalpel or micro chisel. A micro chisel is useful in these situations as it has a smaller contact area than a scalpel blade and is less likely to accidentally cut into surrounding detail.

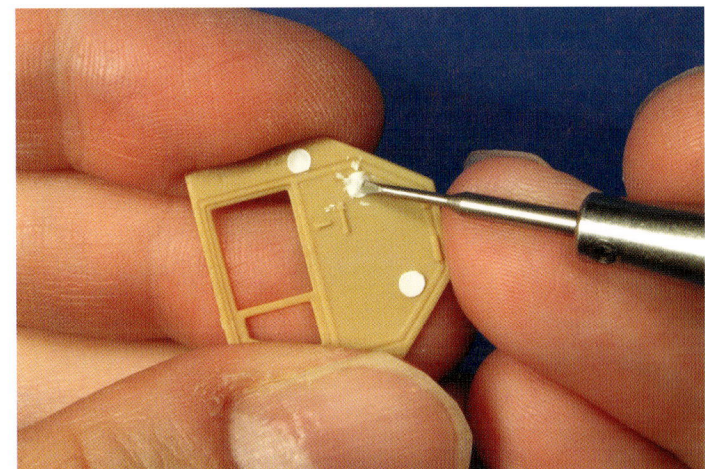

There may still be a gap around the disc, or perhaps it was still a little too shallow to completely fill the hole. In these cases apply some Mr Surfacer 500 to the area with a small brush. Two of the holes seen here have already had this treatment followed by a light sanding down.

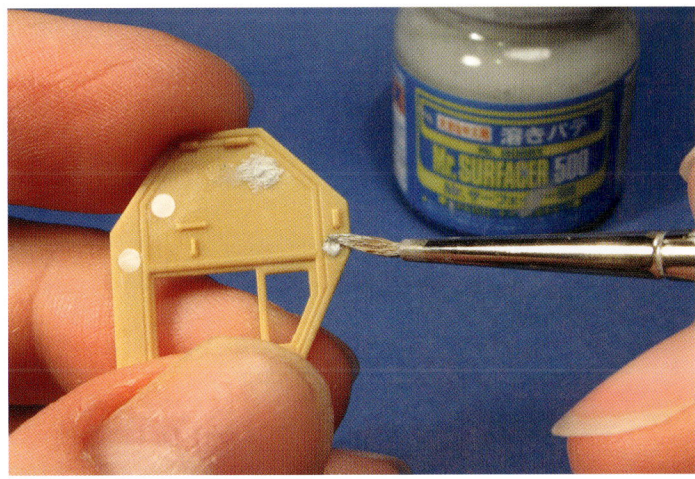

ACHIEVING A SCALE APPEARANCE

The limitations of moulding combined with the smallness of the scale means that parts are sometimes overly thick and unrealistic. This is particularly true of sheet metal items or thin appliqué armoured plate as found on German *Schürzen* for example. In some cases these can be replaced with photo-etched parts if they're available. If not, or for those modellers who aren't too keen on etched sets, they can be made from thin plastic sheet. My preferred thickness for these is 0.25mm. Thinner sheet is available but is quite flimsy and doesn't maintain its shape as well. Any thicker than this and it starts to look out of scale. In fact 0.25mm will normally be on the slightly thick side, but by lightly scraping around the inner edge at an angle, in effect giving a slight bevel, you can get an even thinner look to it.

More complex shapes such as gun shields can be a bit more problematic as they are often composed of several connected plates set at different angles to each other. In some cases it's possible to sand them down, thereby avoiding the need to make a complete replacement or to purchase a photo-etched set. This will require replacement of any surface details but will probably still be simpler than making it from scratch. I take a number of approaches when sanding parts like this down. These include the use of sanding sticks, scraping with a blade and rubbing the part on a sheet of wet and dry paper over a flat surface. Often a mix of these approaches is best and it all depends on the exact size and shape of the part.

The *Schürzen* plates on this early StuG IV were cut from 0.25mm plastic sheet using the kit parts and scale plans as a guide. Thinner plastic is available but there is the danger of the panels warping.

This gun shield is accurate in its dimensions but is too thick. There was very little surface detail to be lost, so I felt the best option was to sand it down to give a more in-scale look to it.

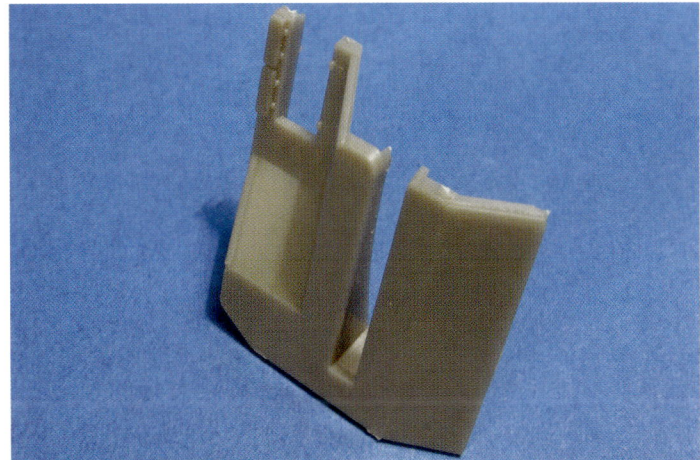

Scrubbing the part face down in a circular motion over a flat sheet of wet and dry paper will slowly thin it down. Try and keep the pressure as level as possible when doing this and constantly check the part to make sure you're keeping the thickness consistent.

The plastic can also be thinned using a scalpel by applying a scraping motion. The tip of the scalpel can be useful in reaching the harder to access areas.

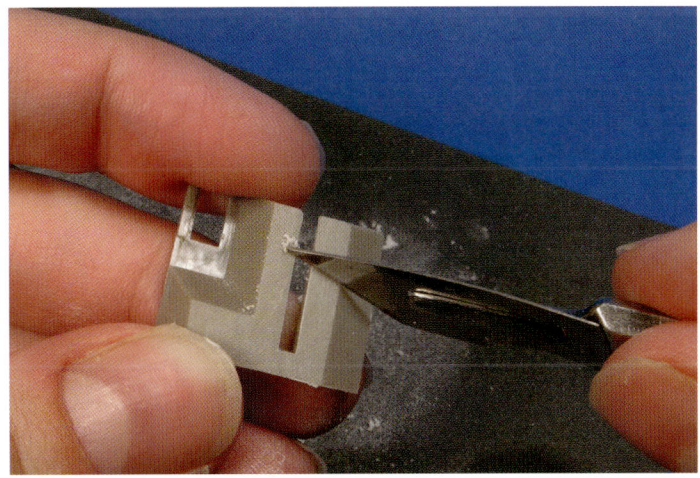

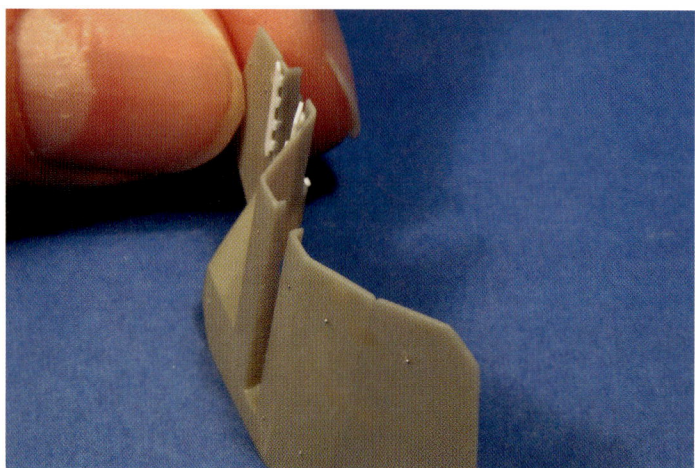

All the faces of the shield have been thinned from the outside and some additional bolt/rivet detail added. Although it requires a fair bit of effort, the results are worth it.

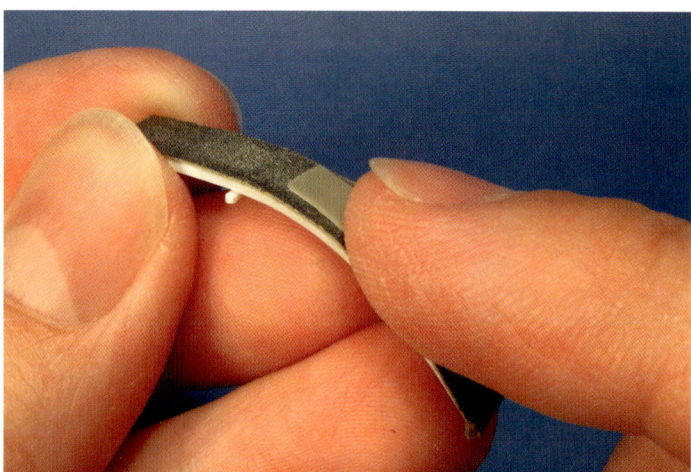

There is a separate curved section to the gun shield that also needs thinning down. For this I made a sanding stick from plastic strip that was bent to the required degree of curvature. Sliding the part up and down this thinned it to a more consistent degree.

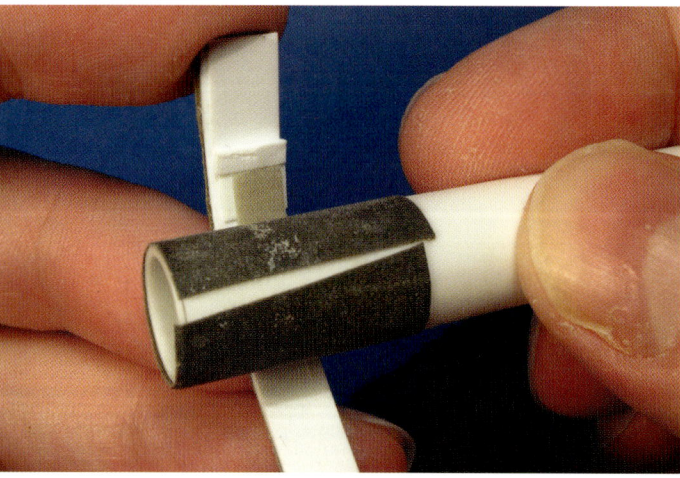

Once the part started to get quite thin I held it against the underside of the sanding strip to make thinning it a bit easier.

The thinned parts look much better on the completed gun.

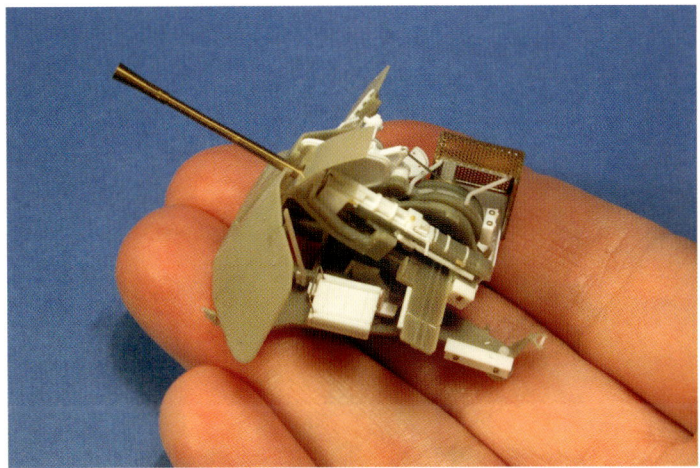

CATERPILLAR TRACKS

Small-scale armour tracks are usually provided in one of two ways: flexible single pieces that wrap around the running gear or as hard plastic links. The hard plastic type is often in the form of single links for the curved sections (such as around the sprockets and idlers) with single piece longer sections for the straight track runs. This type, known as 'link and length', simplifies assembly to some degree and was popularized by Esci in the mid-1980s and later by Revell and others. Some manufacturers, such as Trumpeter with their Famo, have on occasion provided complete single-link tracks that provide the ultimate realism in terms of track sag. This approach isn't particularly common though, with single-piece runs being favoured by Dragon and Revell championing the link and length approach. There are a few manufacturers that take the opposite angle and provide hard tracks moulded integrally with a single piece running gear. This is more common in smaller scales such as the Roco 1/87th-scale range but one of Hasegawa's first

Three common approaches to tracks that manufacturers use are shown here. To the left are link and length tracks from a Revell Nashorn kit. In the middle are individual links from Trumpeter's Famo kit. A small plastic jig is provided to help align these correctly. Finally there's an example of soft, flexible track taken from Dragon's Tiger II kit.

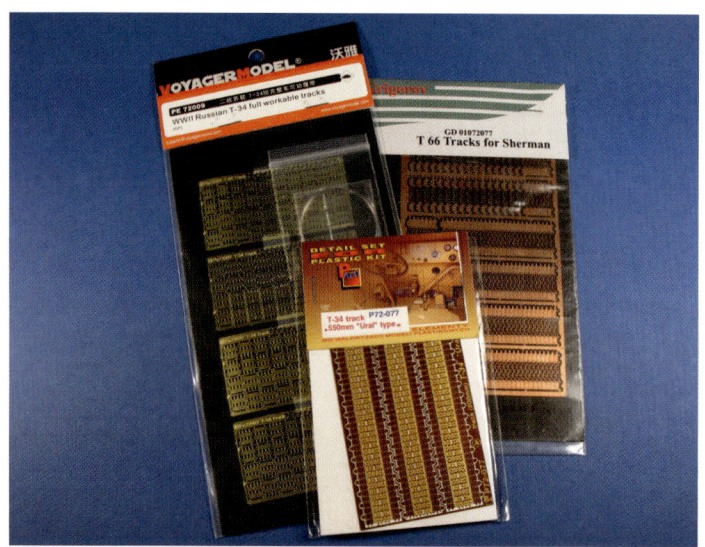

Some aftermarket manufacturers have taken the photo-etched approach to tracks. These are best suited to light tanks with small tracks, or vehicles with thin plate-shaped track links. A few are shown here. The Voyager tracks on the left are even workable and include wire to connect each link. I've not been brave enough to try this type just yet.

A Russian T-26 light tank with photo-etched tracks fitted. The benefit of using photo-etched metal is that the detail is sharp and crisp and track sag is very easy to replicate.

modern vehicles, the Leopard 2, took this approach. The detail on both the tracks and wheels was very poor though and it's only been recently with the resin Combat 72 range from Cromwell Models that

good-quality single-piece running gear has become available.

Another option for tracks is the use of aftermarket sets. This is one area where small-scale modellers aren't served as well as those who

build in 1/35th scale with the options being more limited.

There seems to be an abundance of plastic, resin and white metal tracks sets for the larger scale but far less choice for small-scale modellers. There are quite a number of photo-etched tracks sets available and my own view on these is that they are best suited to thin tracks such as those on light tanks or for plate-like tracks as found on the Russian T-34 tank. There are resin sets around too, some of which require heating of the sections in order to bend them to shape but these can be time consuming and tricky to get right. Some link and length plastic sets are available but there aren't many of these out at the moment.

For kit-provided tracks, I prefer the link and length variety as it's easier to get realistic sag and, unlike some of the flexible alternatives, they take paint and glue with no trouble at all. Many

modellers of small-scale vehicles will have experienced the horror of track melt with some of the older kits from the likes of Airfix and the earlier Esci kits. This will cause paint to fall away and, worse, it can melt the plastic of the wheels where the tracks come into contact with them. A recent innovation from Dragon known as 'DS Styrene' claims to solve these problems. This material does seem to be an improvement in terms of both paint and glue adhesion.

There are several alternatives for approaching the assembling of link and length tracks. I'm always keen to build as much of a model as I can before painting as it means handling the model less once the paint has been applied. Running gear can be completely assembled prior to painting but doing so will make it harder to paint later. If you plan to give it a good coat of mud then this approach may be suitable.

The method I use most often is to assemble the track around the running gear but to only glue the track sections to each other and to the idlers and sprockets. This allows removal of the track and makes painting both it and the wheels a lot easier. As most road wheels appear in pairs, gluing the inner ones to the hull but leaving the outer ones separate will allow you to slide the track away once assembled. It also makes painting the outer wheels easier too. The track joins will be delicate, however, so care is needed when handling them. There are times when I've gone a step further and assembled the tracks without gluing them to the sprockets and idlers. This gives the easiest route when it comes to painting but the tracks are at their most fragile. This is exacerbated because the track runs need to need to have a break at the sprocket area in order for them to be removed from the model.

This Panzer IV/70 (A) has had the track and running gear all glued to the model before painting. I wanted to represent a muddy vehicle so I gave the lower half a stippled covering of ready-mixed model filler first. Since they were covered in mud I didn't need to worry too much about painting the tyres and tracks separate colours later.

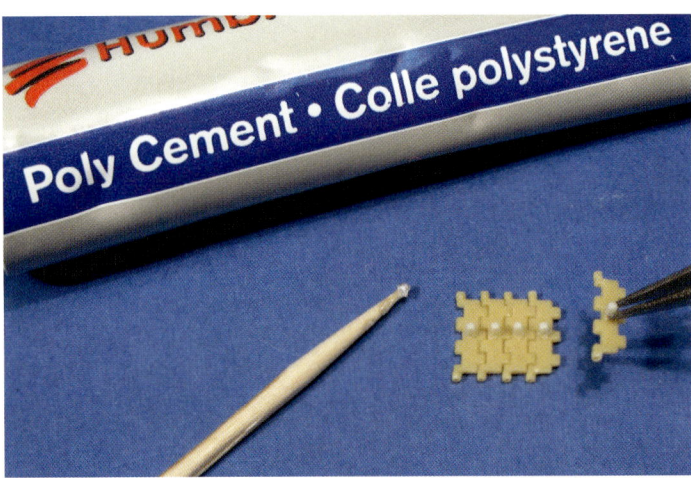

I start by gluing together enough individual links to wrap around the idler. Shown here are links from a Revell T-72 kit that have been cleaned, had the inaccurate guide horns replaced and the track pin ends drilled out. Using polystyrene cement allows some time to work with the completed strip before it sets in position.

Once complete the section can be held steady using metal callipers to ensure all the links are aligned correctly. They can also be pushed more snugly together and will maintain their alignment.

Whilst still workable the section can be glued around the idler. Ensure all the links remains perpendicular to the idler's axis.

The single length of track that runs from the idler to the first road wheel is glued on now, but only to the idler. The lower run of track can be temporarily attached to the wheels with Blu-Tack and glued to the shorter track length. Note that only the inner road wheels are glued to the hull to make both painting and removal of the complete track runs easier.

The next step is to repeat the previous procedure but this time at the rear with the sprocket.

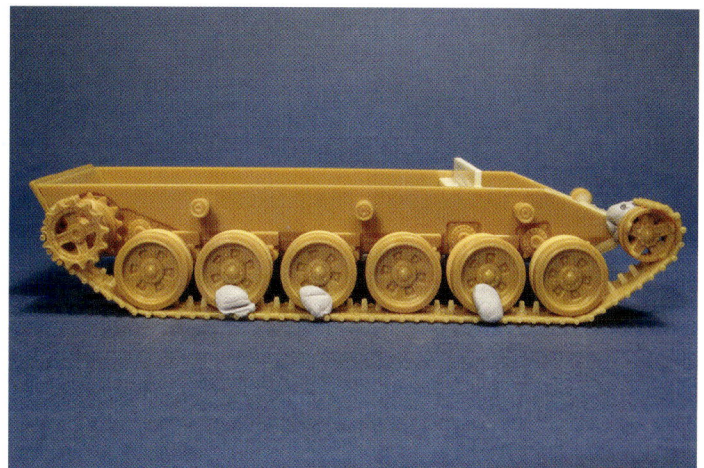

The final step involves adding the top run of track. It may turn out that it is not a perfect fit in between both ends – being slightly too short or too long. This won't be a problem if the vehicle is to have side skirts fitted but if not then a bit of extra work with the idler will be enough to fix the issue. Most real vehicles have a movable idler arm to allow the track tension to be adjusted. Slicing off the kit idler arm and repositioning it should provide enough leeway to fit the top run of track correctly.

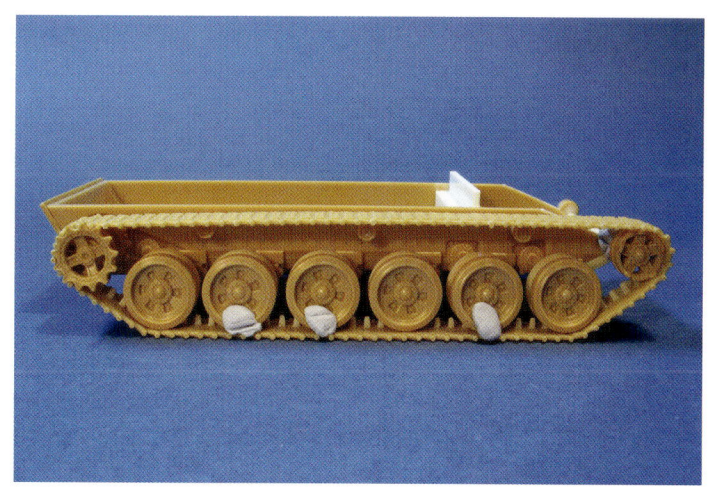

REPLACING KIT GRAB HANDLES

Kit grab handles and rails are usually too thick and in some cases are moulded as solid lumps. Replacing these is an easy way to make a noticeable improvement to a model. Even those that are separately moulded and close to scale will still require careful clean up and due to their frail nature will be easy to crack or break.

If the kit has moulded-on grab handles then these need to be removed first. You may want to note the length of the handle before you do this, unless you have some scale plans to hand to base the new version on. Alternatively I've found that even after removing the handle completely a strip of darker plastic will remain underneath that can be used as a guide. The bulk of the handle can be easily clipped away first using side cutters. Even cutting as close

to the part as possible won't remove the entire handle and I sometimes turn to a micro chisel to get rid of the rest. A scalpel can also be used for this but the narrow cutting surface of the chisel means that accidental damage to surrounding detail will be minimized. If there is still any final residue this can be sanded away with wet and dry paper. This is another instance where I like to use homemade sanding sticks as they can be made in any size needed for almost any task. For the job illustrated in the photos I made one of just the right width to sit between the rivets that sit either side of the handle. In order to make drilling the mounting holes easier I mark their positions by gently pushing a needle or pin into the right locations. Fitting the needle into a pin vice first will make this easier. Now when the holes are drilled the drill bit will be

less likely to slip along the surface of the plastic. I always select a drill bit size that is very slightly larger than the wire diameter as this gives room for the glue. Too tight a fit will more than likely cause the wire to bend out of shape. Once the holes have been drilled I cut a length of L-sectioned plastic strip that will fit just between them. If you haven't any of this available then two strips of plastic of the same length can be glued together at right angles along their lengths. Now's the time to actually make the grab handle. A length of wire (that is at least as long as needed) requires a right-angled bend to be made in it at one end. Holding it in a pair of flat-nosed pliers and then bending the protruding part down with a metal rule is a good way to do this. The longer section of this wire can then be dropped into the channel of the plastic L-shaped holder. The other end of

This truck cab door features a long vertical grab handle moulded as a solid piece. I began by clipping the bulk of it off with side cutters.

Most of the remains of the handle can be removed with a micro chisel or the tip of a scalpel blade. A thin sanding stick is ideal for ensuring the surface is smooth and flush.

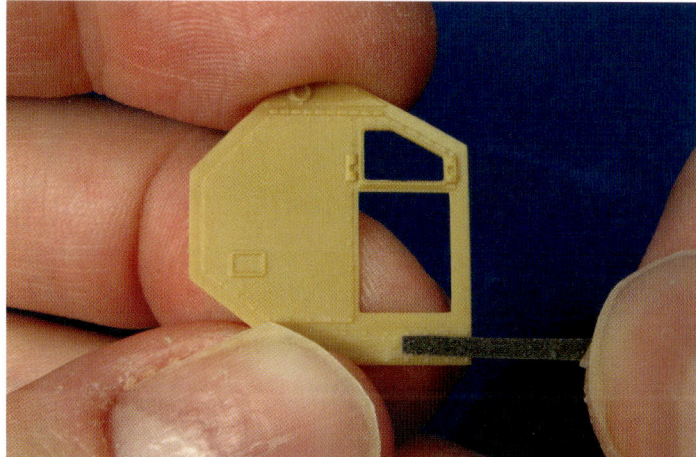

I drilled out holes to accept a new grab handle that I will be making from wire. I usually mark the positions of the holes by gently pushing a pin into the appropriate locations as this prevents the drill bit from slipping.

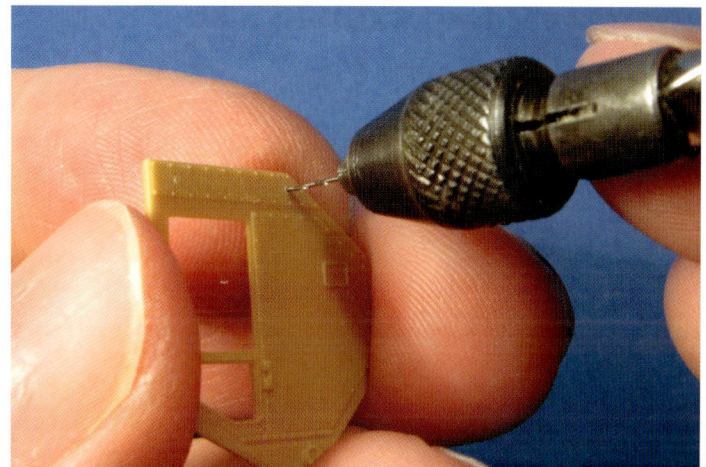

Next an L-shaped section of plastic strip is cut to fit just between the holes.

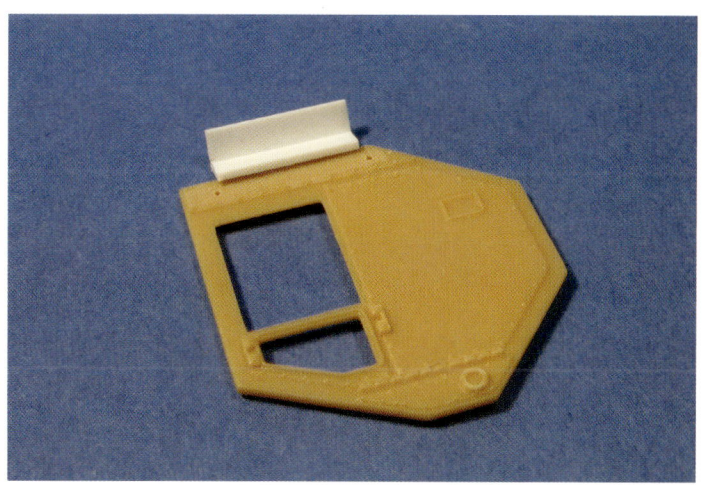

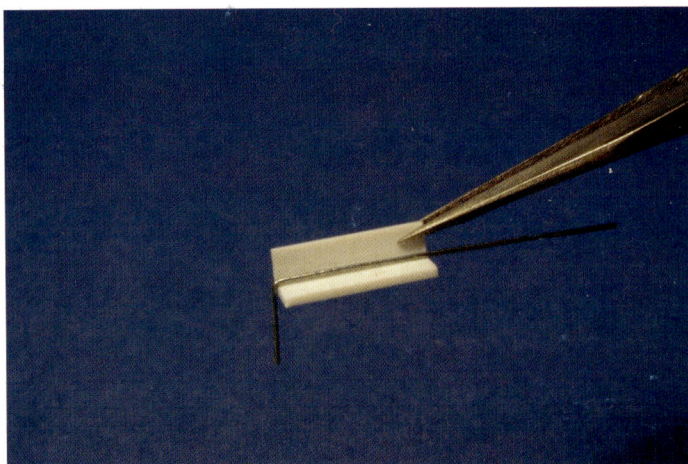

A length of the chosen wire needs to be bent to a right angle at one end and the longer section placed down the channel of the plastic strip.

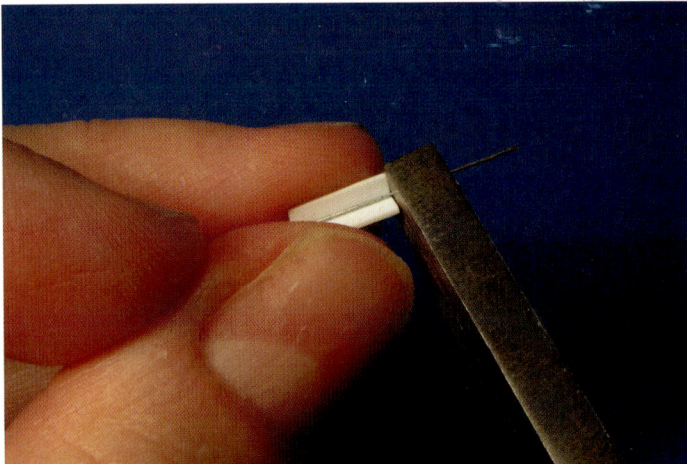

Holding the wire and plastic together at one end makes sure they keep position. The other end of the wire can be grabbed firmly with small flat-nosed pliers.

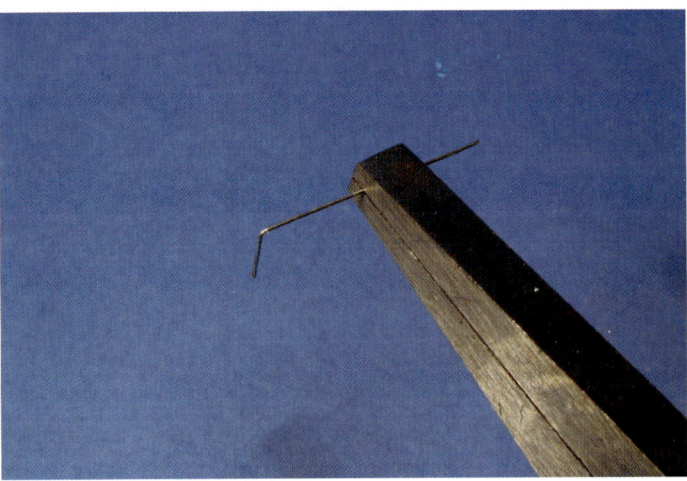

The guiding piece of L-shaped plastic can now be removed to leave the pliers in the correct position for making the second bend.

The second bend can now be made, taking care to keep the whole length of wire all within the same plane. This will give a finished handle ready to be attached to the model.

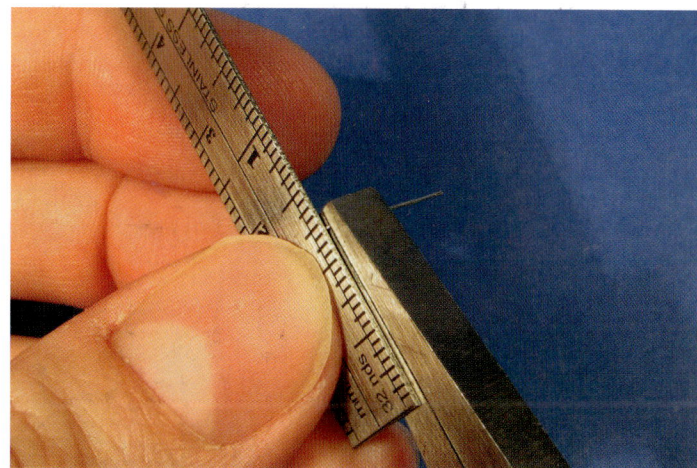

Placing a thin plastic spacer underneath the handle will ensure that it sits at the correct height and that it remains parallel to the surface.

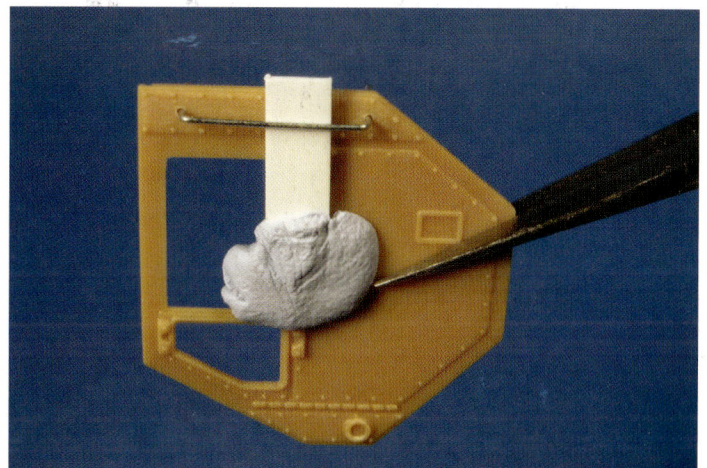

The improved kit part with the new handle fitted. Further copies can now be made if needed.

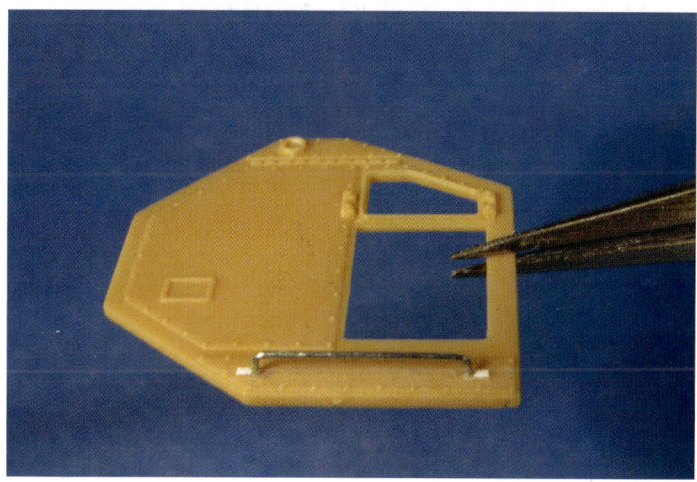

the wire now needs to be gripped with a pair of flat-nosed pliers in preparation for making the second bend. The L-shaped holder can now be removed as it's served its purpose of acting as a guide for the length of the handle.

The two major benefits of this method are that the new handle should be a perfect fit for the holes drilled earlier. It also allows further copies to be made using the same L-shaped template, ensuring each one is identical in size. For this particular model I needed another for the opposite side cab door. After removing the second handle I used the template as a guide for the distance between the two holes that had to be drilled on the other door. The job of attaching the handle still remains and it can be tricky to ensure it sits at the correct depth and remains level with the surface.

To make this easier use a plastic strip spacer of the same depth as the handle height and place it under where the handle will sit. Superglue gel is a good choice for attaching these handles due to its gap filling properties and slightly longer drying time than standard liquid superglue. This will allow you to correct any slight mistakes in the positioning.

REPLICATING CAST-METAL AND RUST EFFECTS

There are occasions when a rough-cast metal finish is required and the kit part may be smooth or have a barely discernible texture. The techniques for achieving this look can also be used to create a rusted finish on items such as exhausts. A popular method for reproducing these surfaces involves

stippling Mr Surfacer 500 onto the surface with a brush. It does tend to dry quickly and so the stippling action has to be quick, although additional layers of Mr Surfacer can be applied later. For this method I use a cheap old brush and, once done, remove the excess putty with liquid polystyrene cement. For small parts I use just a fine round brush and for larger items a flatter brush is more suitable.

Creating a cast-metal appearance can be done in a very similar way using Mr Surfacer. When doing this I use more of a dragging motion, rather than stabbing the brush against the part. Again some light sanding at the end can reduce the strength of the effect if it looks a bit overdone. This technique is particularly useful for vehicle with cast turrets, such as those of Soviet and Russian origin.

Mr Surfacer 500 is ideal for achieving a rusted effect on exhaust pipes and cylinders. Stipple it quickly by rapidly stabbing at the surface.

Once the Mr Surfacer has set hard, it may require a light sanding to smooth it off a little. You can also apply more Mr Surfacer to further deepen the effect.

The finished exhaust has a nice flaky texture to it. This will really come to life when painted.

A cast effect has been achieved on this tank turret by dragging Mr Surfacer over it. Although similar to the process done to achieve a rusty effect, this results in a flaky appearance.

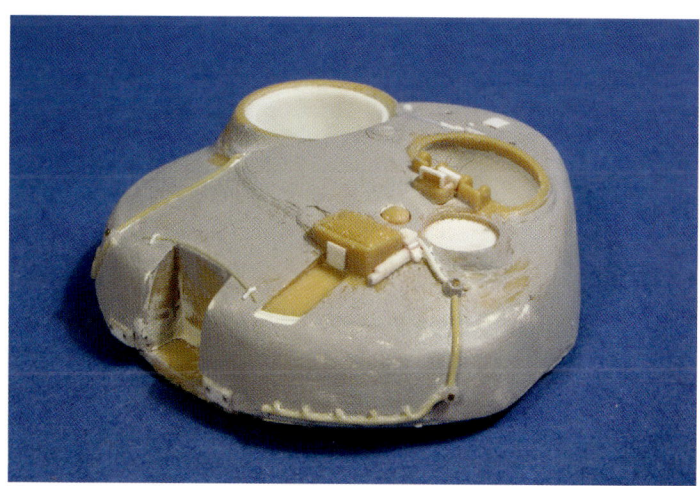

MAKING REALISTIC HEADLIGHTS AND MIRRORS

Creating reflective surfaces such as those found in lights and mirrors is always a challenge as painting them in metallic paint never looks particularly realistic. The headlights provided in most kits are almost always solid plastic items and will never look that great no matter how they are painted. A few companies sell clear plastic lenses in different sizes that have a far better appearance, with both the glass front and reflective rear being realistically represented. I have a small collection from the MV Lenses range that I purchased at a model show in the USA a couple of years back. Items such as this used to be hard to find sometimes, but with the advent of the Internet and online ordering from overseas it's not such a problem these days.

Fitting the replacement lenses is straightforward and just requires drilling out the solid plastic one. Marking the centre with a pin or needle will make it easier to get the drill bit centred initially and will also prevent it slipping once you start drilling. I would never use an electric drill for this type of work, no matter how low powered, as

I selected some appropriately sized headlights from the MV Lenses range.

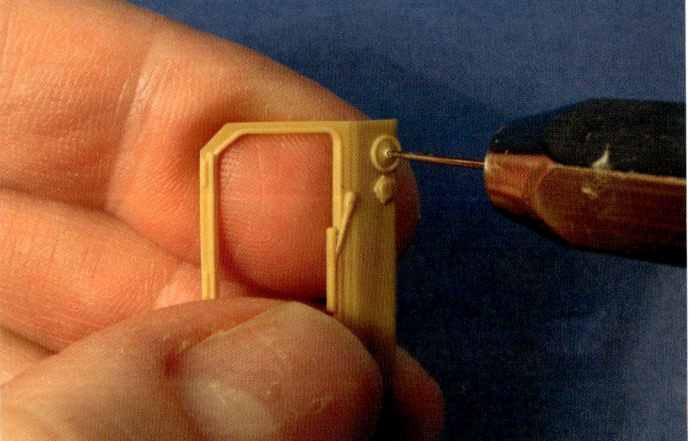

Marking an impression at the centre of the light is important for keeping the drill bit in the right area. You can do this by pushing a pin into it to leave a small guiding hole.

The kit light has now been drilled out and the process needs to be repeated on the other side.

The new light is test fitted and sits well. It can now be left separate from the model and glued in place once the model has been painted and finished.

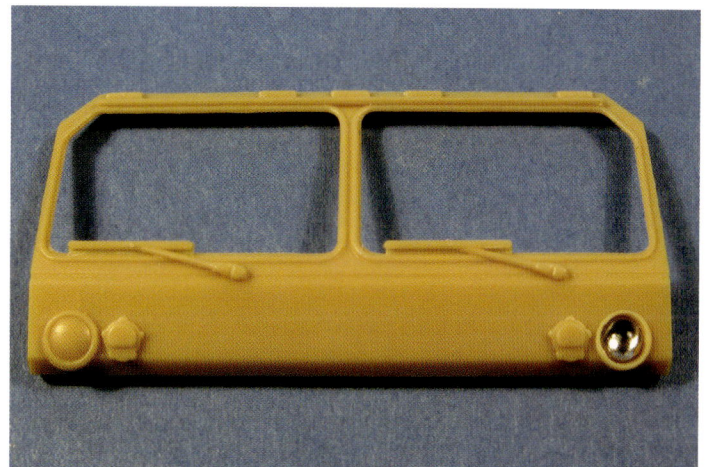

These wing mirrors are very small and it's difficult to get a really close photo of them that does them justice. They're made from the inside of plastic foil chocolate bar wrappers. These have a good reflective surface but don't crinkle in the way metal foil does. I attached these once the model had been painted with white glue. If any glue overspills it can be wiped off with the corner of a damp cloth.

drilling it manually is easy and less likely to damage any surrounding detail. Once the holes have been created the model can be built and painted with the lenses just being dropped in with a little glue to hold them as the very last step.

Most softskin vehicles will be fitted with mirrors and, if done well, they can really enhance a model and add an extra touch of realism. I tried metal foil a couple of times when experimenting with methods and although it had a realistic shiny look it had a propensity to wrinkle. A much better alternative is something that I already had in the house, especially with two children around. Many chocolate bars these days are packed in a plastic foil that has a similar appearance to metal foil but doesn't crease or wrinkle. This can be cut into small strips of the appropriate size and simply attached with some white PVA glue once the model has been painted.

IMPROVING WINDSCREENS

An area of particular relevance to softskin vehicles is that of glass parts such as windscreens and side windows. There are a few ways that kit makers have dealt with these kinds of parts. Some kits contain a clear plastic sprue for the windows, in a similar way to the rest of the kit just with a different kind of plastic. In other cases a strip of thin acetate is included that may, or may not, have the outlines for the windows marked on. The modeller then has the task of cutting the shapes out. Not surprisingly there are pros and cons to each approach. The first approach where hard plastic versions are provided has the benefit of the items being ready shaped. They just require snipping from the sprue and a bit of the usual clean up. On the negative side these parts are invariably too

thick or even worse may have scratches and other surface imperfections due to the moulding process. Thin acetate will give a much clearer and realistic glass appearance at the expense of a bit more effort in getting there. This is my preferred solution, and in those cases where the manufacturer has provided hard plastic parts I'll replace them myself with acetate.

Sheets of acetate can be purchased from office stationery or art shops but I've collected several spare ones from kits that have included far more than is needed for a single model. The kit items can be used as a template around which thinner copies can be cut from the acetate. A good way of doing this is to use a pencil to draw around the kit piece onto a piece of plain paper. Try and keep the pencil as close to the edges as possible to avoid creating a copy that is too large. I use a mechanical

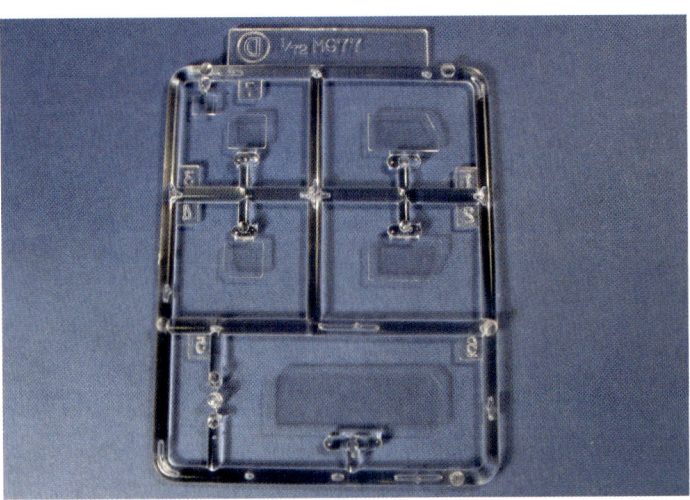

The glass parts in this kit are included on a clear plastic sprue. In this particular case they were quite thin but didn't quite capture the look of scale glass.

After being removed from the sprue, each part can be drawn around with a pencil on plain white paper. Try to keep as close to the original size as possible.

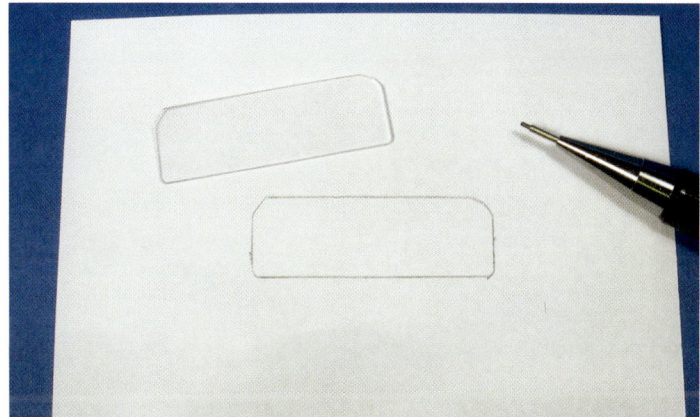

The frame can be cut out with a scalpel held against a steel rule. Curved corners are a bit tricky but can be cut manually with some practice.

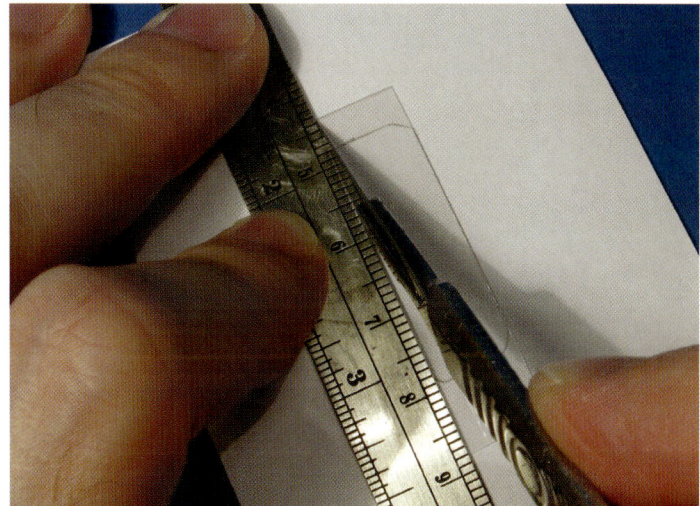

The finished piece should be a simple drop-fit into the window frame. It can be stored somewhere safely whilst the rest of the model is finished and attached later with white PVA glue.

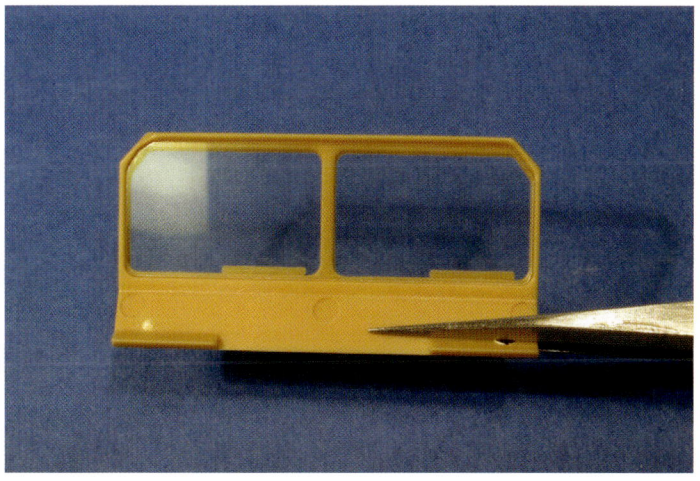

pencil available from art and graphics shops for this as it has a lead that keeps the same, thin diameter all the way down allowing for precise strokes. Once this is done a strip of acetate can be placed over it and the pencil template underneath used as a cutting guide. Even for simple rectangular windows, drawing them onto paper first gives a useful guide for cutting the acetate versions. Straight edges can be cleanly cut against the side of a steel rule and for many windows this will be enough. If the edges are rounded then one option is to cut these freehand although thin metal templates can be found at art shops that usually have many different sizes of curves, holes and other shapes. Very similar to these are model aircraft panel scribing templates that some model and hobby shops sell.

An area where particular care is needed is when attaching clear parts to the model. Accidentally marking them with glue can be disastrous and difficult to put right. I use white PVA glue mainly because it dries transparent. Also being water soluble it's easily cleaned off when dry and won't give rise to the clouding effect that superglue vapours can sometimes lead to.

VEHICLE STOWAGE

Most military vehicles, especially those in action, will carry some degree of external stowage. The amount will vary from vehicle to vehicle but I think it's an important consideration that can add a lot of interest to a model. As well as adding extra realism, a model will benefit from the extra splashes of colour and detail that stowage will add.

Unlike on-vehicle tools that are covered a little later, it's rare to find stowage included in kits as standard. Some of the old Esci kits contained the odd item such as a rolled tarpaulin or two but they weren't very good. So it's down to the modeller to decide on the amount of stowage, if any, that they want to include with a model and where to source it. There is a lot of scope for making your own but there is also a lot of opportunity in the aftermarket area with there being a great range of resin sets available. Most of these contain far more items than are needed for a single model and so collecting them over time will give rise to a good selection of different parts for future use. Common types of stowage include spare ammunition boxes, crates, tarpaulins, jerry cans, tow cables and fuel drums. There are also the

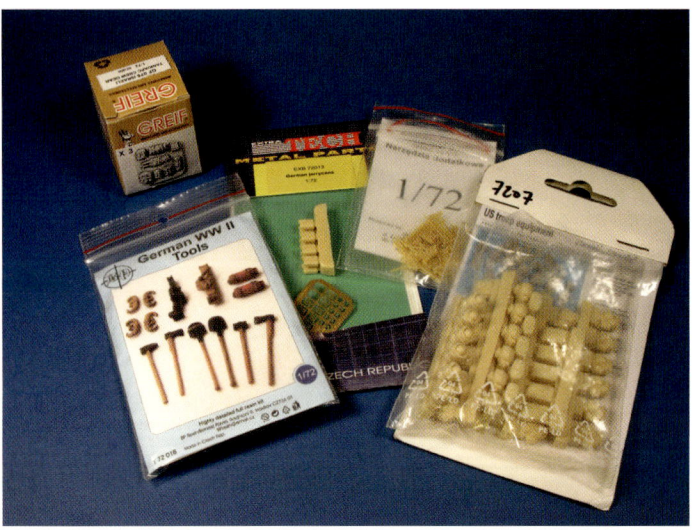

Some examples of resin stowage and tools available to buy as aftermarket items. These are from a number of different manufacturers.

This halftrack has a full cargo bed. Vehicles such as these are crying out for plenty of stowage, otherwise they end up with a large and empty rear that doesn't attract the eye.

Some vehicles can be seen with spare track piled up around the front to add extra protection. The spares box is a good source for these parts. On this particular example I added some track from a different vehicle to add an extra little touch.

Years ago the most realistic way of creating tow cables was to use fine nylon thread. Nowadays you can buy pre-twisted copper cable in many sizes to help you make your own. You can even buy dedicated tow cable sets with resin cable ends included.

crew's personal items such as kit bags, helmets and ration boxes amongst other things. All of these can be found in resin sets or can in some cases be easily scratch-built.

Many military vehicles carry tow cables and some kits ignore these completely or provide them as hard plastic parts. I've never encountered any plastic versions that have looked particularly realistic and as they are pre-formed to shape they often don't fit well. They are usually fiddly to clean up too. In the good old days the most realistic way of creating replacements was to use fine nylon thread that had a characteristic twisted appearance to it. After drilling out the kit tow cable ends you could glue sections of the thread in to give a nicely flexible tow cable. These days though you can buy twisted copper cables in many sizes to help you make your own and these are soft enough to bend into a realistic

shape. In fact there are tow cable sets targeted at specific vehicles available now, notably from a company called Eureka XXL. These sets have resin cable ends that are pre-drilled and also the lengths of twisted copper cable of the correct diameter.

CREATING TARPAULINS

I'm going to take a look at creating your own tarpaulins using two-part epoxy putty rolled into thin sheets. In the particular example I use here I'm going to make a single piece that will be draped against other items of stowage in a truck cargo bed. Once this technique is mastered there is no end to the variety of shapes and sizes that you can create at will. Rolled-up stowage, bags and other soft materials can be easily reproduced in miniature and the small amount of putty needed makes it very cost effective too.

MagicSculpt epoxy putty is my favoured type for making tarpaulin and other similar items of stowage. I only mix small amounts, enough to make either a few or perhaps even just one tarpaulin. This allows enough time to make each one without rushing before the putty starts to harden. I work over a plain white ceramic tile that can be purchased from hardware and DIY shops. This has a very hard, smooth and perfectly flat surface that is perfect for rolling putty on. Rolling the putty into a thin sheet is similar to rolling out pastry and has the same issues of the material sticking to both the surface and roller. Whereas flour is used to prevent this when working with pastry, odour-free talcum powder is a good solution for putty and it can be sprinkled in a thin layer over the tile first. Once the putty has been mixed I roll it into a ball and then squash it into a disc

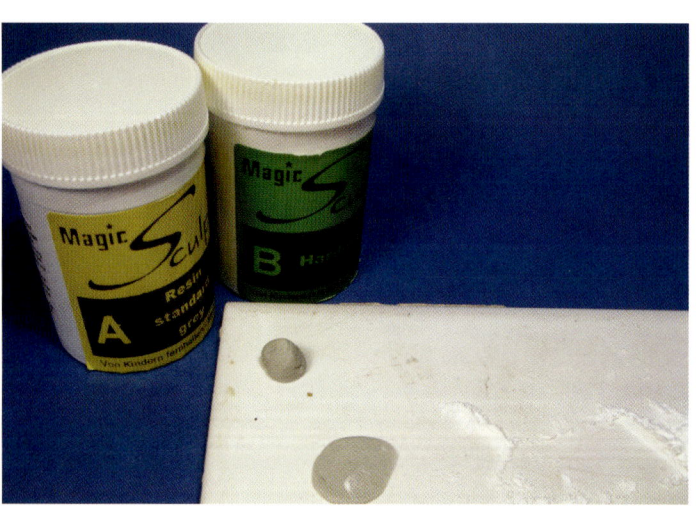

I mix some MagicSculpt putty and sprinkle talcum powder over a smooth flat surface such as a ceramic tile. This will help to prevent the putty sticking to it.

Sprinkling talcum over the putty too will help prevent it sticking to the roller. Note the two plastic strip spacers that ensure the rolled sheet has a consistent thickness.

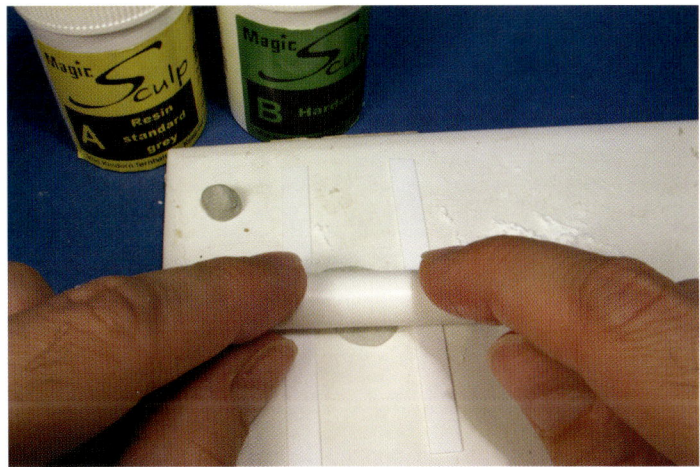

Once the putty has been rolled flat, the edges can be trimmed away to leave a rectangular piece.

Even with plenty of talcum powder you will need to take care when peeling the putty off the tile. It can now be carried over to the model.

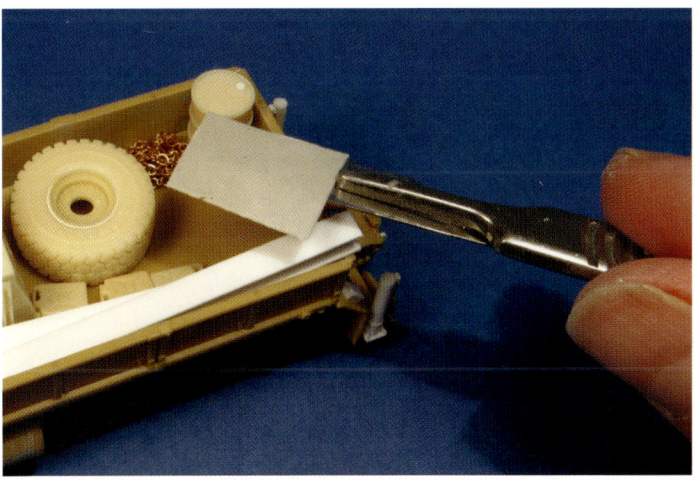

Using a cocktail stick with the end rounded off, I start to create folds and creases by gently pushing the putty against the stowage items sat near it.

Once the creases and folds have been made the putty needs time to harden.

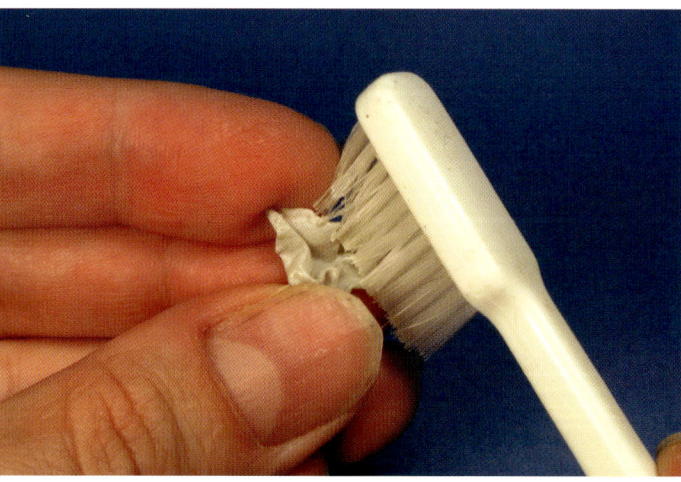

I brush off excess talcum powder with a soft toothbrush. Doing this will help the paint adhere much better.

shape onto the tile. Applying some more talcum powder on top helps avoid it sticking to the roller. The roller itself is just a length of wide plastic tube. I sprinkle powder over this too but if it gets bits of hardened putty on over time it can just be thrown away and replaced. One of the difficulties is getting the rolled sheet to a consistent thickness and this can be overcome by laying a couple of plastic strips of the desired thickness either side of the putty. When the roller reaches these it will have given a uniformly thin sheet. It's wise to apply more talcum powder occasionally, especially if the putty starts to stick to the surface or roller, as this will keep the sheet from tearing. Trimming the edges and removing the excess putty will give the final piece that can then be worked with into the final shape. It can be rolled up to form bedrolls and other similar things or just kept as a flat sheet to drape over the vehicle. In both cases wrinkling and folds will need to be added and for this I use a cocktail stick with the ends rounded off. Until it sets the putty will remain quite fragile so it needs to be handled delicately whilst working with it. Any damage will be difficult to repair so it's worth taking things

slowly to avoid this. Once the required shape is achieved and the putty has hardened it's also important to clean away any excess talcum powder. The very first time I used putty in this way I didn't do this. In fact there wasn't really any talcum powder visible but it had formed a very thin, almost waxy layer over the part. After applying a coat of paint it started to rub away when adding highlights and shadows and wouldn't adhere properly. Scrubbing with a soft toothbrush will do the trick in removing this and the surface will then accept paints well.

On-vehicle tools

On-vehicle tools that are found as standard on the real vehicle are different from other types of stowage as they usually will be included in the kit. The best kinds are moulded as separate parts but often they are moulded directly to

the model. When provided in this way they are both harder to paint and in many cases less realistic. I've seen examples that are far too flat with little relief and barely any undercuts. Thankfully there are a number of solutions to these problems. It may be possible to replace the tools with some from the ever-present spares box or failing that either scratch-build them or use aftermarket sets. Resin tool sets are available from several manufacturers and there are also some photo-etched sets that contain tools. I've never actually used photo-etched items for these situations though as the tools appear too flat and unrealistic in most cases. This is especially true for items such as shovels and other tools with a cylindrical handle or element to them. Photo-etched parts will never be able to match the appearance of plastic or resin equivalents.

Photo-etched sets sometimes contain parts for the tools. Unless the real items are flat then these are unlikely to look realistic.

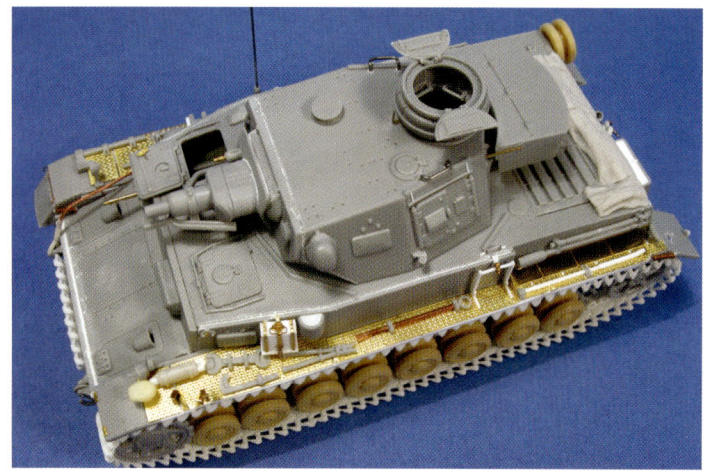

Dragon's Panzer IV Ausf. F contains a mix of moulded-on and separate tools. I cut the fenders off and fitted plastic strip replacements. These were covered in tread plate sections cut from a photo-etched sheet. I salvaged most of the moulded-on tools by cutting them off the discarded fenders which also gave the opportunity to improve the undercuts that they lacked. A few of the items are from resin sets, such as the Notek light and fire extinguisher body. I-created a few extra ones myself using plastic rod, strip and copper wire.

This Revell Panzer III also had the tools moulded to the fenders. This is an example of a kit where the tools are far too flat in shape and can't really be salvaged. Once I'd replaced the fenders with photo-etched versions I replaced most of the tools with ones from the spares box along with a few homemade ones.

For smooth fenders and surfaces the tools can be just cut off and the surface sanded flat. Fenders that feature any sort of tread plate pattern pose more of a problem as it will be almost impossible to remove all of the tools without damaging the pattern underneath. In fact the area directly under the tools won't have any pattern there once the tools have been cut away. There are many photo-etched fender sets available that can be used in these cases and usually the tread pattern in these are better than that found in the original kit. Some of them also include the complete framework to support the tread plate but I usually don't bother using these and simply remove the kit fenders to replace them with an equal sized plastic strip. The tread plate can then be glued directly to this and the resulting fenders are a bit sturdier than all etched versions. Rectangular sheets of 1/72nd-scale photo-etched tread plate are also available with different patterns such as lozenge, dot and others. Strips cut from these are more economical than buying separate individual fender sets – but require a bit more work of course than using the pre-cut versions.

ADVANCED CONSTRUCTION TECHNIQUES

There is no clear divide between the skills required for basic and advanced model construction. In fact there are many shades of grey between building an out-of-the-box kit and creating your own fully scratch-built model. Many of the techniques I look at in this chapter would clearly be considered more advanced, but even these can be applied to simple kit builds. Replacing a poorly detailed or moulded part with a scratch-built version can really improve a model and prove to be a very satisfying element of model making.

IMPROVING KIT PARTS

A common issue particularly relevant in the smaller scales is that of oversize details. In Chapter 2 I looked at ways to thin overly thick kit parts but for more complex pieces it may be necessary to replace some or all of the part in order to achieve a better appearance. Some details may not be present at all or may be inaccurate and in all these cases the modeller's only option will be to replace the item.

Trying to cover every type of improvement that can be made to the huge variety of different kit parts isn't possible and would need a whole series of books this size. So I'm going to take a look in detail at a couple of specific examples along with brief descriptions of some others. These two examples look at opening out solid and simplified

kit parts to give a much more realistic appearance to them.

HOLLOWING OUT A COMPLEX EXHAUST

Revell's T-72 tank kit has a solid exhaust piece that lacks the grille-shaped opening at the front. Unlike a solid gun barrel, this can't

be simply drilled out and requires more effort to get a realistic appearance. The following photos illustrate how a few simple steps can give a more complex-looking part. In fact no matter how complex a part is, it can always be broken down successively into more manageable chunks.

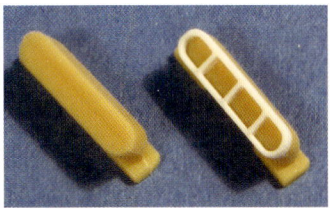

Right: The exhaust on the left of the picture is moulded as a solid piece but should have a grille-shaped opening. The improved piece is shown on the right. Its shape makes it a bit more of a challenge to reproduce than a simple circular or rectangular hole.

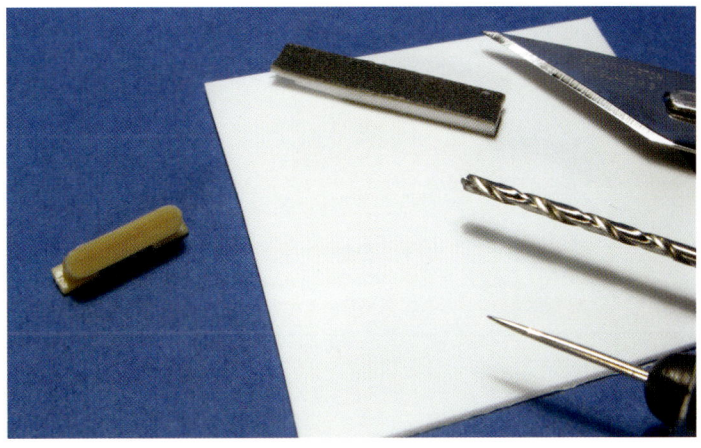

Right: The tools and materials that we will need to modify the part are shown here. They include a sanding stick, scalpel, drill bit, pin and some plastic sheet.

The rounded ends of the opening can be made by drilling holes of the required diameter. Mark two guide holes first with the pin at the centre points of these. The location of these can be worked out by taking the overall width of the opening minus its height.

The central part of the opening is removed by cutting two slices across the gap between the two holes.

Time to pop the central strip out – the basic shape of the opening is now apparent.

The straight edges of the opening need a bit more attention to make sure they are parallel to each other and also the correct distance apart.

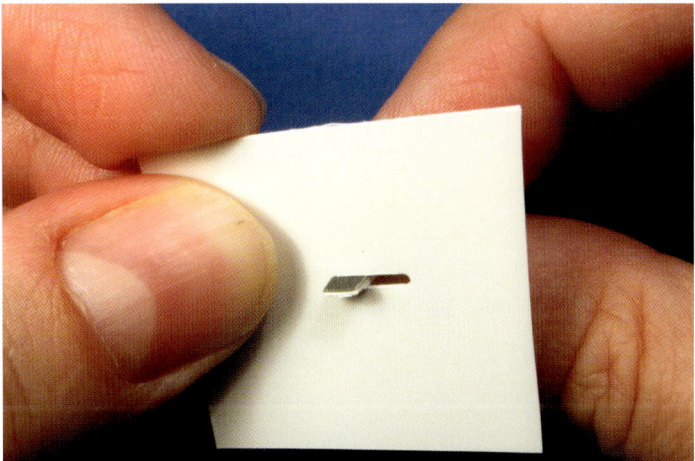

The opening has now been trimmed to a more manageable size. The kit part has had its solid face cut down by an amount that matches the thickness of the plastic sheet.

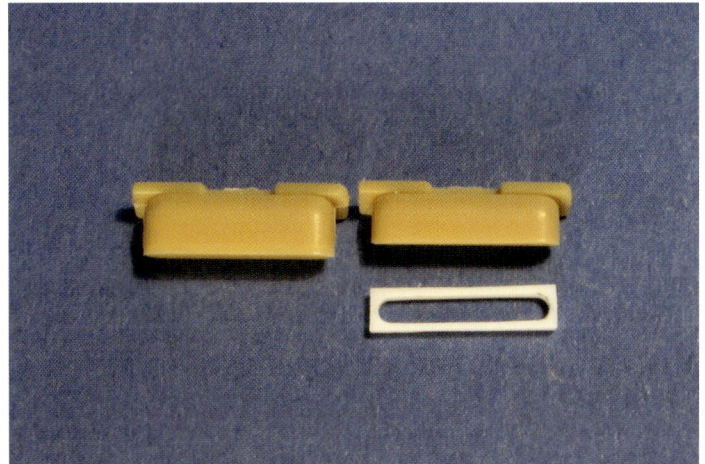

After gluing the roughly trimmed part to the exhaust piece I sanded around it to ensure a seamless fit.

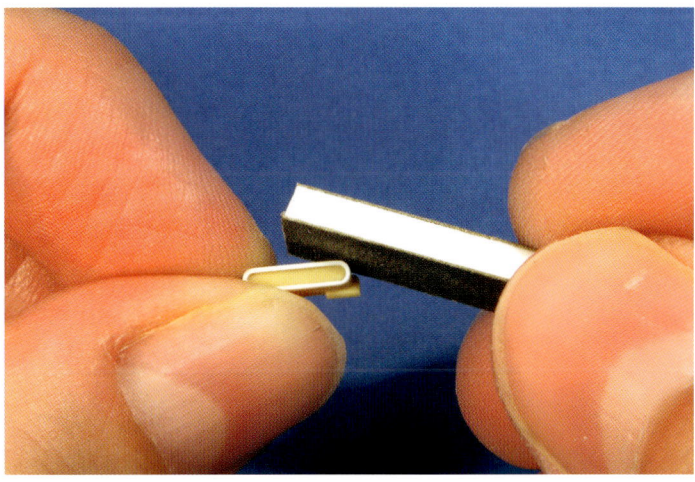

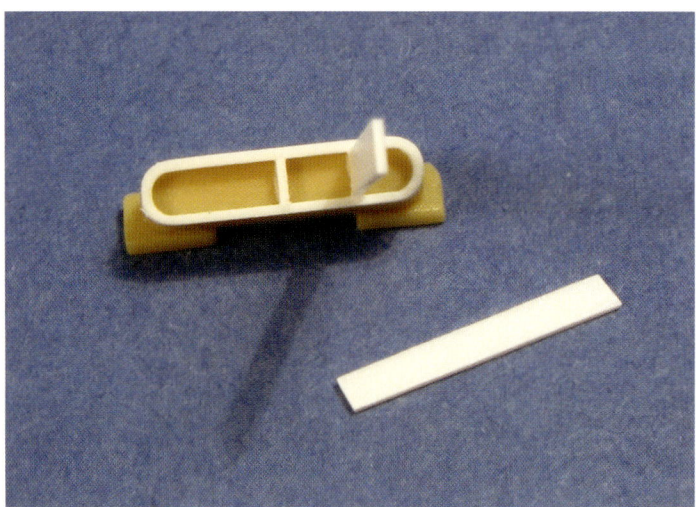

The vertical grille sections are added next by gluing plastic strips into the opening and trimming them so they sit flush. Once done the modified exhaust piece was complete. As I planned on building several models with this type of part I went on to create some resin copies. Home casting will be covered later in this chapter.

IMPROVING A KIT EXHAUST

The M977 HEMTT truck kit from Academy provides a single-piece exhaust with perforated sheet metal guard around it. Being moulded in one piece results in a lack of depth to the perforations and the gap between the sheet and the exhaust is missing. This is one of the trickier kinds of part to fix but with a bit of effort isn't as difficult as it may at first appear. Visualizing the gradual breakdown of the part and the steps to get to the final result will come quickly with practice.

The exhaust piece in Academy's M997 truck is moulded as a solid item. This gives it a simplified and unrealistic appearance that can really do with some attention.

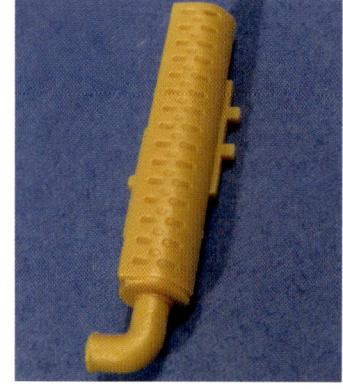

The approach I took here was to remove the cylindrical body of the exhaust leaving just the curved metal sheet portion. I began by clipping the bulk of the exhaust away with side cutters.

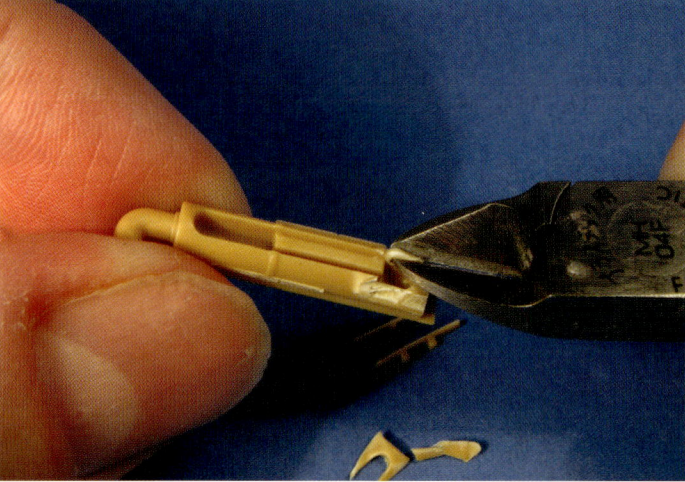

A micro chisel is useful for removing more material before sanding the remaining section away.

A bevelled or round cross-sectioned needle file is very handy in these cases to remove the rest of the plastic.

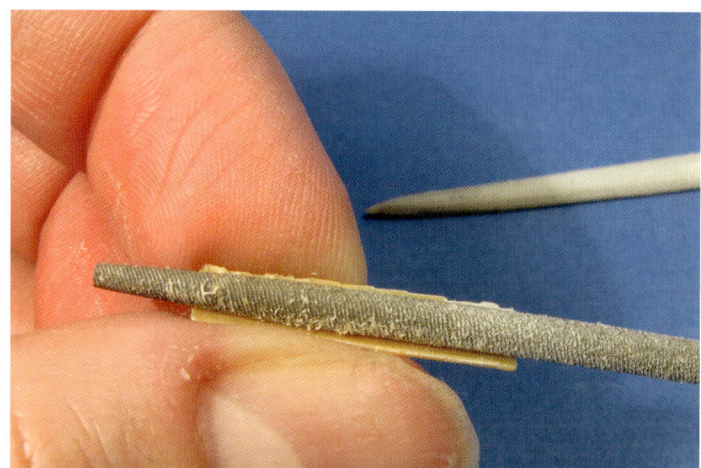

The perforated exhaust guard is now at a reasonable thickness and the solid holes can be opened out. As the part is a bit more fragile now, supporting it with a cylindrical sanding stick ensures it doesn't get bent or damaged.

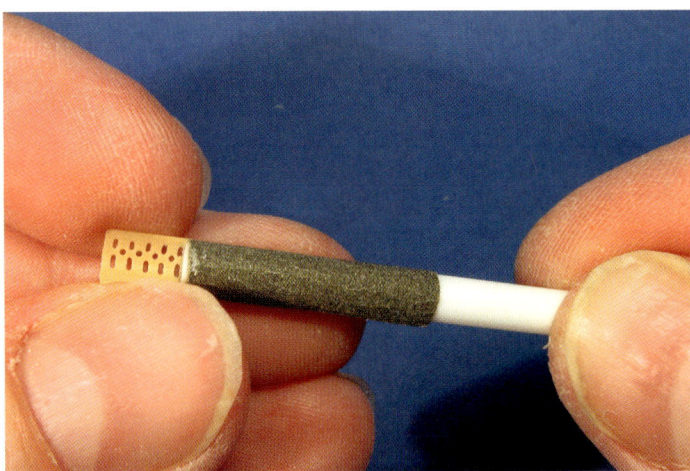

Running the sanding stick along the rear of the piece and giving it a quick brush with an old toothbrush will remove any straggling bits of plastic.

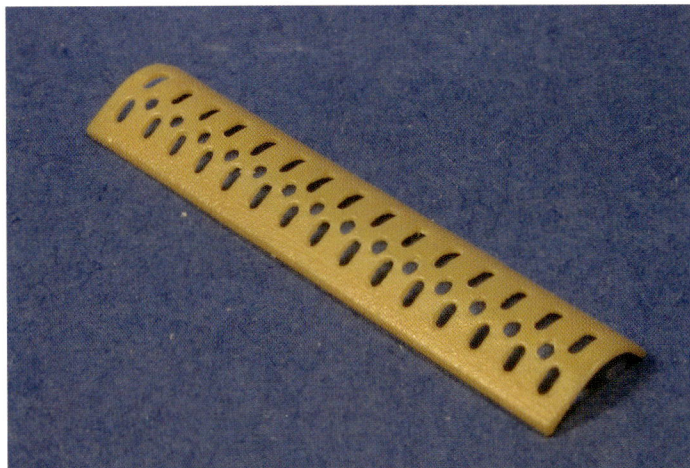

The new guard is a big improvement on the solid kit piece. Now the exhaust itself needs to be replaced and this is the easier part.

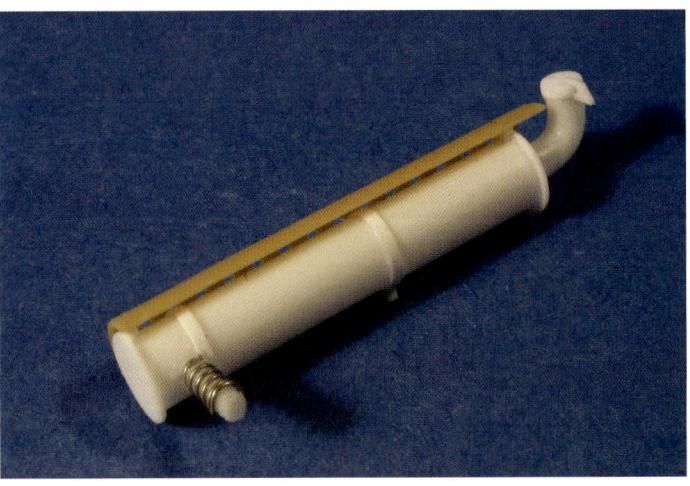

The completed exhaust assembly. The main body is just a section of plastic tube with the ends sealed with plastic discs. The smaller fittings were just made using plastic strip and heat-stretched plastic rod for the curved pipe.

RIVETS AND BOLTS

There are many occasions when I find myself looking to create my own rivets and bolts. This is particularly true for conversion and scratch-building work but can also be the case when working with standard kits that may be lacking them, or have had some damaged when cleaning the parts up. There are many approaches to doing this and I've probably tried most at some time or another over the years. Even now though I don't just use a single method – some may be more appropriate than others under different circumstances. Whatever approach is followed, creating tiny rivets or bolt heads in small scale is challenging due to their size. I'm going to take a look at some of the common techniques for doing this but focus more on the ones I use the most.

PUNCH AND DIE

The punch and die set was discussed briefly in Chapter 2 and the smallest hole on most sets can be used to create larger-sized 1/72nd-scale rivets and bolt heads. The main benefits of this approach are speed and the consistent thickness of the discs. For most types of rivet though the results are just that bit too large. A variant of this technique is to use a pin or needle with the sharp end sanded slightly flat. When fit into a pin vice this can be used to punch small discs from a thin sheet of plastic placed over a rubber mat. It can work well but without the help of a surrounding die the ratio of well-formed rivets to those that are unusable is quite high.

EMBOSSING

Rather than producing individual rivets, this method embosses or imprints rivets from the reverse

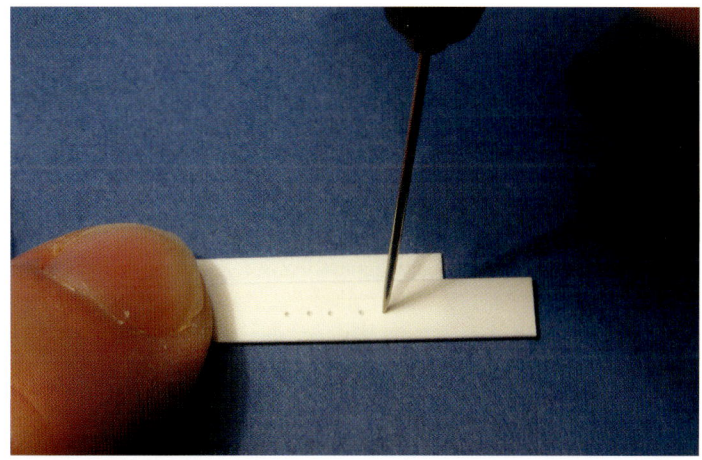

A blunt needle fitted to a pin vice can be used to emboss rivets from the reverse side of thin plastic sheet or strip. Having another piece of plastic or a firm rubber mat underneath is also necessary, as a surface that is too hard will prevent the rivet forming properly.

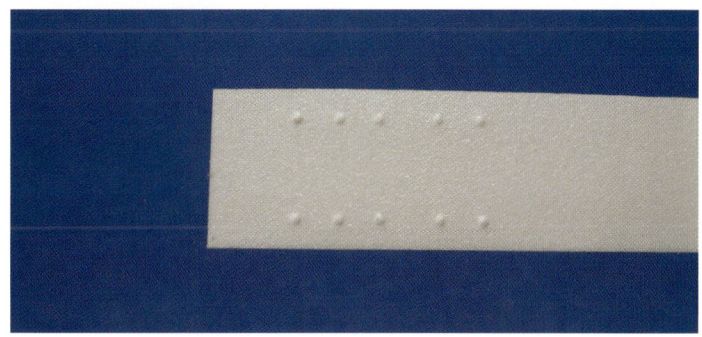

A number of rivets have been pushed through this test piece. The technique requires practice in order to consistently create rivets of the same depth and to avoid pushing too far and piercing the plastic.

side of a thin sheet of plastic. I've found this solution to be useful during scratch-building when I've been creating the structural parts as well as the rivets themselves. The resulting rivets are also domed shaped rather than just flat discs as a punch and die set would produce. I use a blunt pin held in a pin vice to impress the pattern and after marking the positions out the pin can be gently pushed into the plastic at each point a rivet is required. The best way to do this is to apply minimal pressure to avoid cutting through the plastic and ruining the effect. Having a firm rubber mat underneath is also necessary, as a surface that is too hard will prevent the rivet forming properly. If the surface is too soft it won't support the plastic very well and it will bend and buckle. The tricky part of this method is firstly getting the rivets properly spaced

as once one is created it's not as easy to remove it cleanly again. Also the depth of the rivet depends on the pressure applied so getting this consistent across all of the rivets requires care and practice. I've found a good way to solve the first problem is to use a piece of photo-etched, rectangular-holed mesh to act as a template and guide. I have a number of these with different-sized holes and I can usually find one that is of the correct dimensions. For the other issue practice is the main way to solve it. Plus applying less pressure to give a shallower rivet isn't a problem as it's easy enough to repeat the procedure to deepen it. When a satisfactory set of rivets has been made the plastic can be laminated at the rear to give it added strength. I use superglue gel for this as it will also fill the small hollows at the rear of each rivet giving them a bit of extra strength.

PLASTIC ROD AND STRETCHED SPRUE

One of my favourite methods of rivet making requires lengths of plastic rod or sometimes heat-stretched sprue. Slicing rivets off the end is a simple procedure and with a bit of practice a scalpel or razor blade can be used freehand to do this. Usually I take this approach when only making a few rivets, and for more than one you can glue plastic rod sections lengthwise at one end. A set of rivets can then be cut in one go. A slightly different approach is to mark small holes with a pin at the location of each rivet and drill a hole out at each of these locations. Sections of plastic rod can be inserted into each hole and pushed through until the desired height is achieved. A small blob of superglue applied at the rear of the surface will hold the rod in place and then the excess can be trimmed away.

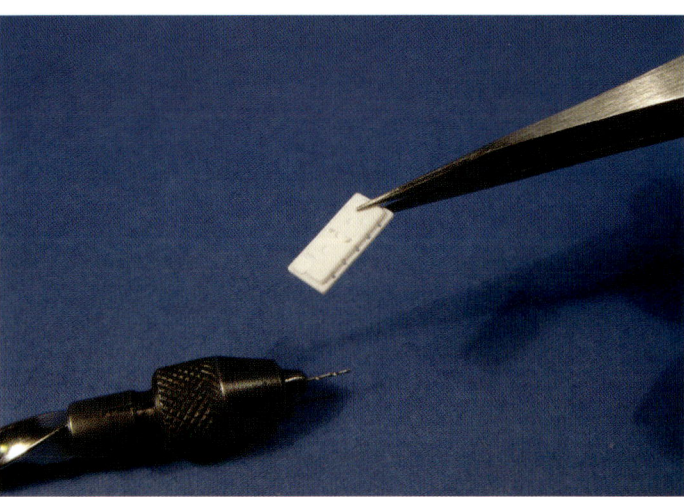

Fitting lengths of thin plastic rod to pre-drilled holes is one of my favoured methods of making rivets and bolt heads. After marking the positions of the rivets the holes can be drilled out.

A small blob of superglue gel placed near the top of a section of plastic rod will hold the finished rivet in place.

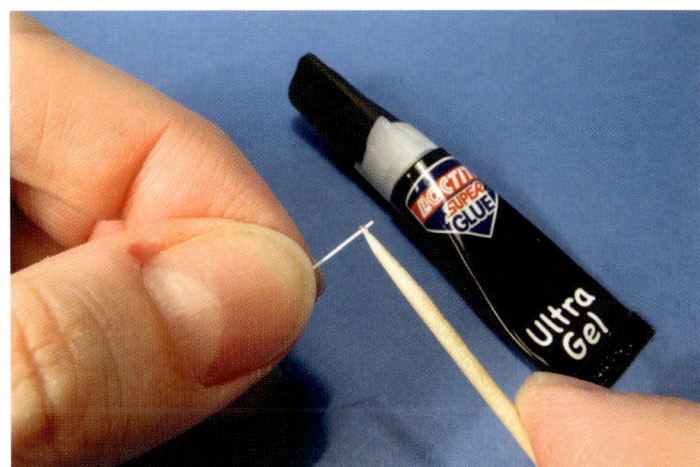

Inserting the rod from the underside of the part will ensure no glue gets on the top side. Once the glue has dried you can trim the underside away. When all the bolts have been added they can be lightly sanded from the top to ensure a consistent height.

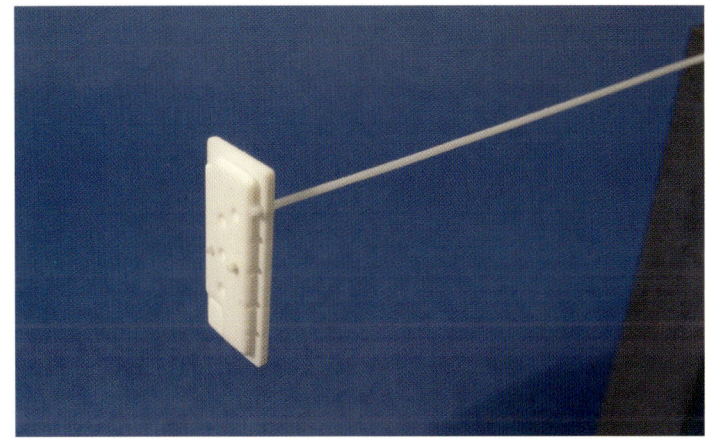

Gently sanding the surface of these rivets with a sanding stick will ensure they all sit at the same height. I like this approach as the rivets will remain firmly on the model and won't be knocked off either during the rest of the construction phase or when painting and weathering the model.

THE NUTTER

Apart from the punch and die set there is another specialist tool that can be used for mass-producing rivets. This is the Nutter, available from The Small Shop, and consists of a punch, a number of interchangeable heads that screw into it, some metal sheets and a sturdy base unit. Details for obtaining this are given in Chapter 8. The base unit has a small flat rubbery section on top of which the foil is placed and a clamp holds it in place. The punch is then used to just push through the foil, knocking out a flat rivet, domed rivet or even an open nut depending on the selected punch head. Although there is no die part, the foil is cleverly designed to avoid the need for this. Rather than being a single layer of metal, it's actually three different laminated layers containing a lead core sheet. The surrounding layers allow for safe handling whilst the softness of the lead helps to give well-formed rivets. The smallest-sized domed ones are very small indeed and perfectly sized for many uses on small-scale

The Nutter is a specialized tool for making tiny bolts and rivets that I introduced in Chapter 2. The thin laminated metal sheets are secured to the base unit and sit over a rubber mat. They can be punched out using a firm degree of downwards pressure until you hear a click as the rivet is made.

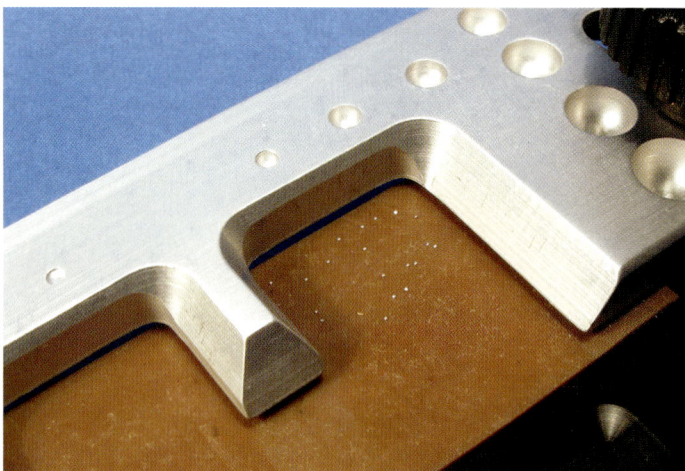

The rivets get embedded into the rubber mat and can be gently removed with the tip of a scalpel blade.

To attach the rivet I use either superglue gel or two-minute epoxy glue. I tend to use superglue when I'm confident I can get the rivet in the right place the first time. The slower-drying epoxy glue gives time to reposition and is ideal in cases where it's more difficult to get the right position straight off. I apply the glue to the part with a sharpened cocktail stick. I've marked this end of the stick with a pencil.

Dampening the other end of the stick will allow you to temporarily pick up the rivet and place it onto the glue.

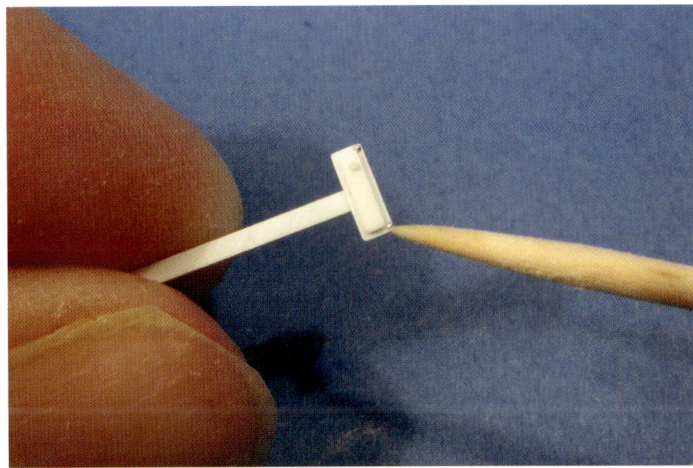

The tiny size of the rivets can be appreciated here.

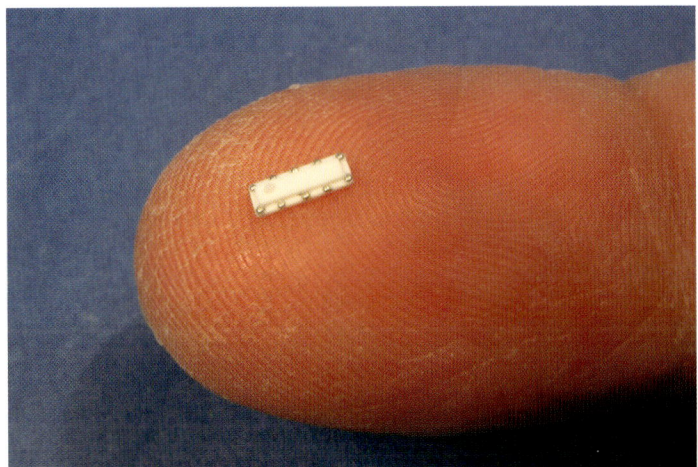

This part shows a combination of the two methods I rely on the most – the Nutter and plastic rod/sprue method.

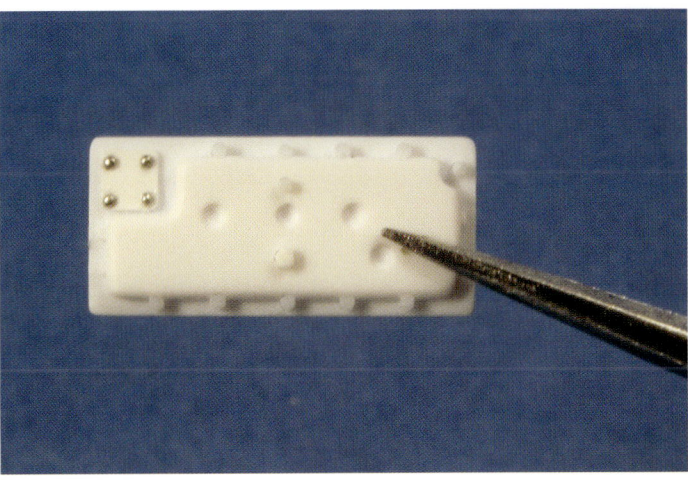

models. A good way to attach them to the model is to dab a small blob of epoxy glue on the surface and place the rivet on top. The hollow dome shape means that the glue fills the interior and when dry gives the rivet strength. This also gives good adherence to the surface of the model. The downside of this method is the high cost of the initial unit and the ongoing cost of the metal sheets. Having said that the sheets provided in the initial kit have lasted me a long time and this method is my favoured one for the smallest-sized rivets and bolts.

OTHER METHODS

There are other methods of making rivets but some of these I've only tried once or twice, or not at all in some cases. This isn't to say that none of them are any use, just that the ones I've just described in more detail work well enough for me so far. There are some photo-etched sets containing rivets and bolts in multiple sizes and shapes and I've made use of the hexagonal type on a number of occasions. Slicing rivets from another kit is an old method of sourcing rivets. This is probably more suitable in larger scales and has the downside of the cost of the original donor kit. Another method involves the use of 3D paint to dot the rivets onto a surface. This type of paint is designed to create relief effects but after trying this out I found it wasn't easy to achieve consistency in the size and shape of rivets. Another method uses dry transfers. Archer are a well-known source of dry transfer markings and also have a range of surface detail transfers including rivets, tread plate and weld beads.

MODELLING GERMAN WORLD WAR II *ZIMMERIT*

Anyone who's interested in German armour from the latter half of World War II will probably have built a model at some point that required *Zimmerit*. Although my intent for this book is that it will contain hints and tips for modelling in general, creating *Zimmerit* is a challenge that many modellers will face at some point due to the popularity of the subject. *Zimmerit* was an anti-magnetic mine paste applied for a period during the latter half of the World War II, being discontinued before the end of the war. It was usually applied on vertical or sloped surfaces rather than horizontal ones and the intent was to prevent magnetic mines from sticking to the sides of vehicles. Photos show it was

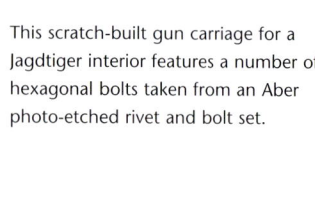

This scratch-built gun carriage for a Jagdtiger interior features a number of hexagonal bolts taken from an Aber photo-etched rivet and bolt set.

almost always patterned in some way and there were many different type of this. Two common ones were the ridged pattern and the waffle pattern. Of these the ridged pattern is probably the one modelled the most and this is the one I'll be looking at here. There are several options for representing this in 1/72nd scale, far more than were available many years back when the only option was to make it yourself.

COMMERCIAL PRE-MOULDED *ZIMMERIT*

Some of the more recent plastic kits, notably from the Dragon range, have *Zimmerit* pre-moulded onto the parts. I've generally been impressed with this as the kits I've seen have shown an often accurate and in-scale pattern. A minor down side is that representing damaged *Zimmerit*, with chips and missing sections, is a bit more difficult than with some of the other

methods. Also when not done well it's impractical to try and remove it all for an alternative solution.

Thin sheets of resin *Zimmerit* are available that a modeller can cut panels from and these can be applied to both flat surfaces and those that curve slightly along one axis. This doesn't solve the problem of those cases where it needs to be applied to compound curves though. Some resin sets aimed at specific vehicles solve this by

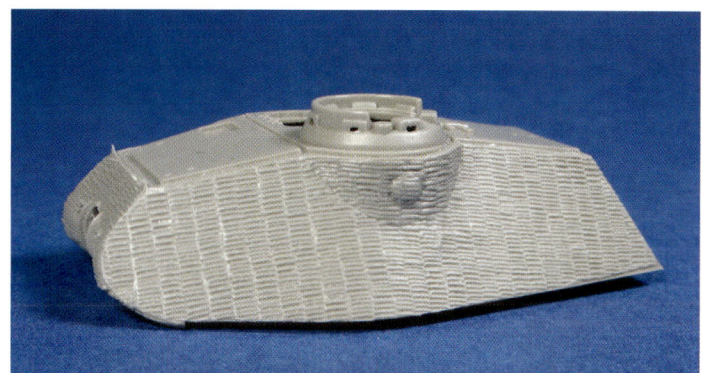

Some injection-moulded kits have a *Zimmerit* pattern engraved on the parts, saving additional work for the modeller. This is Dragon's Porsche Tiger II turret and the pattern is very well done.

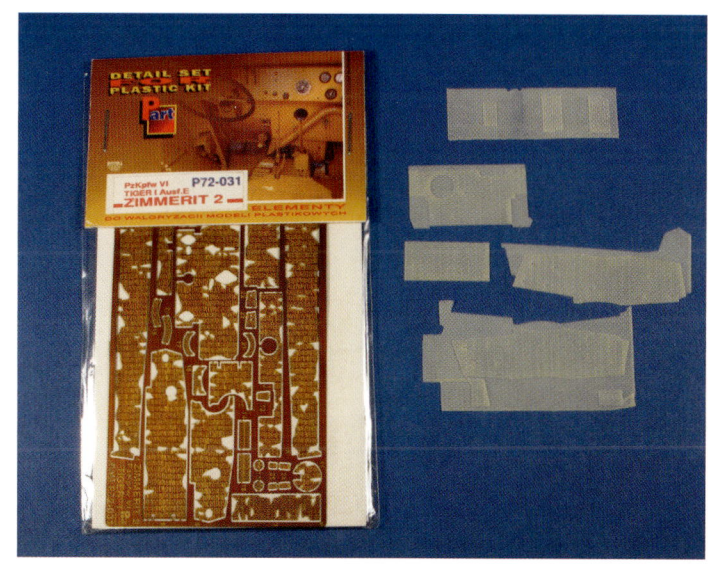

Two common approaches for aftermarket *Zimmerit* are photo-etched sheets and resin. A problem with photo-etch is that it's only suitable for flat parts or those that are slightly curved. Resin sets often come as a mix of sheets along with whole replacement parts for more complex shapes.

providing a mix of flat sheets and completely moulded parts for the occasions where those parts are more complex in shape.

There are also a number of sets made for individual vehicles done as photo-etched pieces. These are generally restricted to slab sided vehicles due to the inflexibility of the medium around compound and tight curves. I prefer the resin approach over photo-etch as the etched type is naturally very flat looking. Although thin, *Zimmerit* has some relief to the ridges that photo-etch just doesn't reproduce well.

HOMEMADE *ZIMMERIT*

Making your own *Zimmerit* used to be the only option available and there are two common approaches that I'm aware of. The first involves imprinting the pattern directly onto the model using either a heated screwdriver head or a small pyrogravure. A pyrogravure is just an electrically heated needle that can be used to shape soft materials such as plastic. It can be used to engrave the characteristic *Zimmerit* ridges into the surface of the model. The other option requires a thin application of putty to the model and the pattern can then be imprinted with some form of *Zimmerit* tool. I favour the latter approach for a number of reasons. The pyrogravure method leaves very little room for error as it directly affects the surface of the model. It's also hard to represent realistically chipped *Zimmerit* this way. Real *Zimmerit* has depth of course and, although very thin at this scale, the pyrogravure method won't give this effect. For the second approach my preferred medium is Milliput epoxy putty. Its long drying time leaves plenty of scope to fix errors and to even remove it all if you're unhappy with the result. Once dry it is very hard and durable but can be realistically chipped away just like the real thing. As always there is a negative and achieving a thin enough, uniform layer can be a challenge but one that I don't think is beyond the capability of most modellers.

To start I roughen up all the surfaces that will have an application of the *Zimmerit*. Doing so gives the putty a better surface to adhere to, preventing it from flaking off when set. A coarse piece of wet and dry will do the trick and scouring the surface with this will give it a rough feel. I often score some criss-cross lines over the surface too just to give it an extra bit of texture. One of the keys to creating realistic *Zimmerit* is to get a scale thickness. For small-scale models this is thin indeed, but epoxy putty is resilient and pliable enough to make this possible. I've seen and attempted a few different ways of getting a good coverage over the years. For flat, featureless surfaces I've tried rolling out a thin sheet of putty, draping it over the area and further flattening and

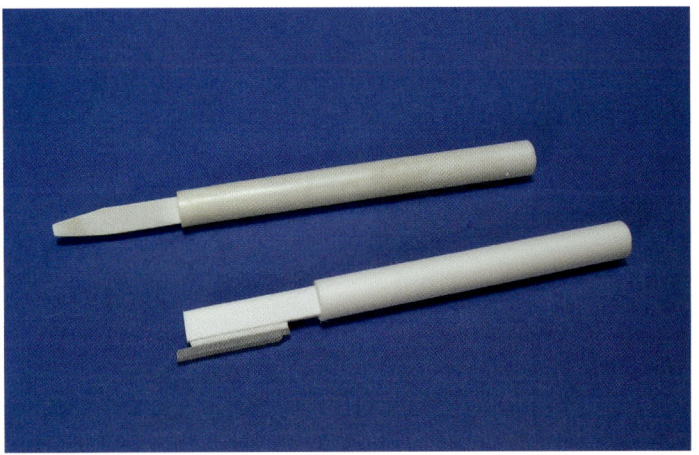

I've used a couple of homemade *Zimmerit* tools for many years now and they've served me well. The first one, to the top of the picture, is just a plastic chisel made with a piece of sanded plastic strip and a plastic tube handle. At the bottom is a thin strip from the edge of a CD case fitted to a makeshift handle.

Roughening up the surface with coarse wet and dry paper will give the putty something to adhere to.

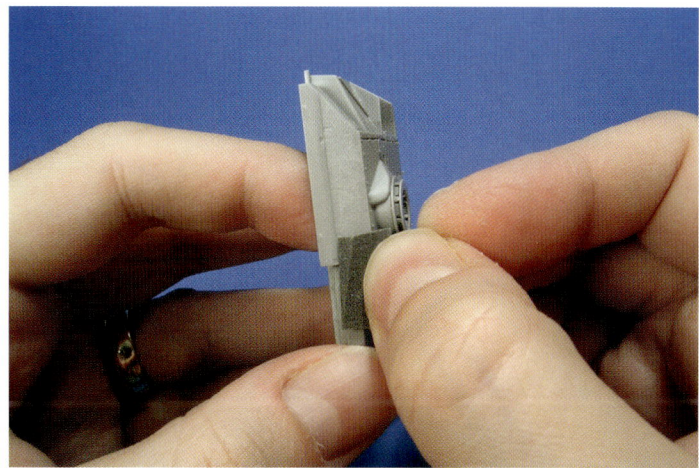

I apply the mixed putty with an old, blunt scalpel blade by pressing down and forcing small pieces of putty flat onto the model.

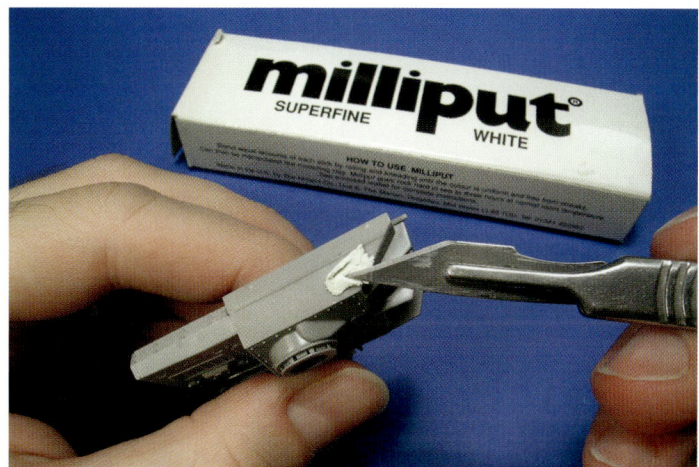

Smoothing the putty off should be done with the scalpel blade liberally covered in water. Using plenty of water ensures it doesn't pull away from the surface.

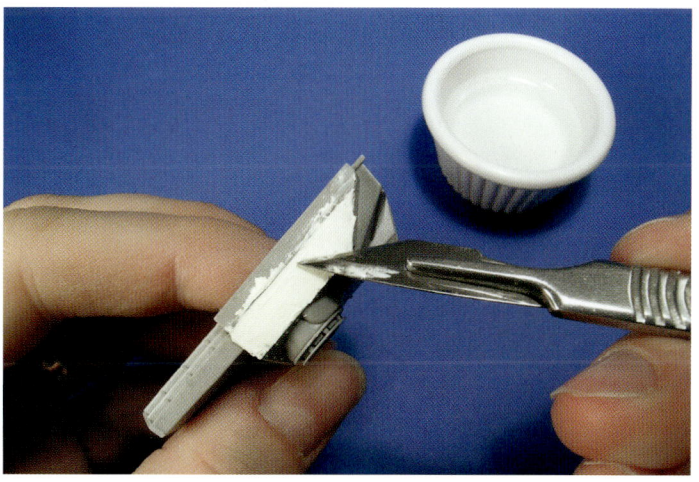

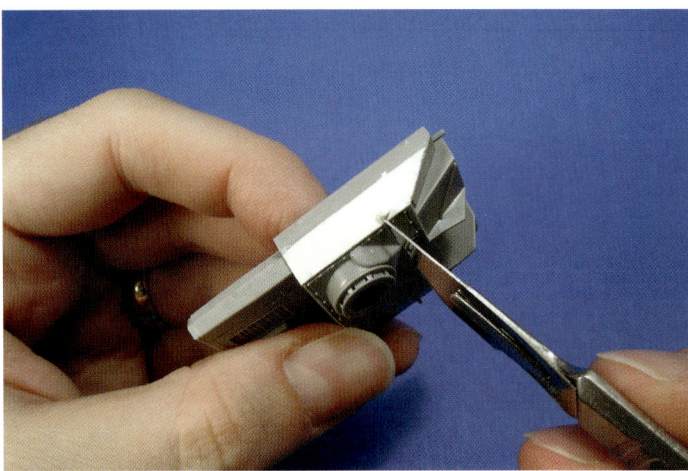

Any excess putty hanging off the edges can be sliced away.

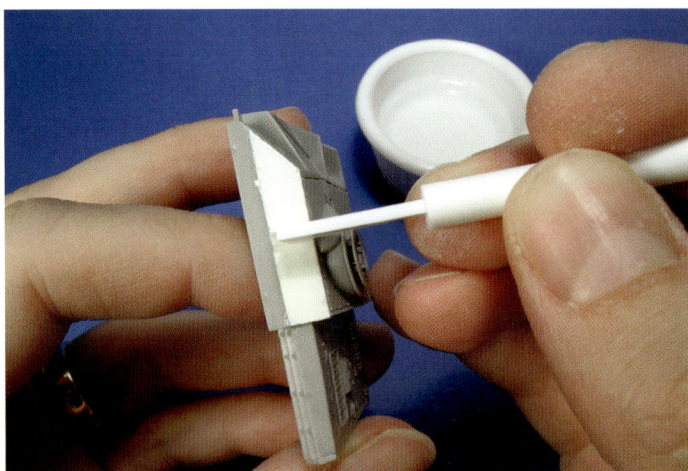

With a nice smooth application of putty in place, the next step is to start imprinting the pattern onto it. For this I use the tool made from a strip of CD case edge. This creates a single column of ridges at a time and moving along the model will build up the full pattern.

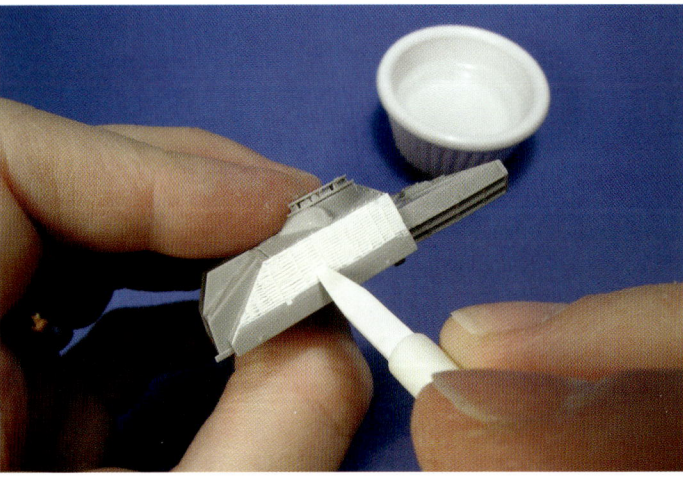

The previous step creates all the ridges but they look too uniform. The chisel shaped tool can then be used to deepen these ridges and give them a more natural, rougher look. Once this is done and the putty is dry, a light sanding is sometimes necessary to remove any particularly rough bits left over.

then trimming it. I don't take this approach any more and now apply small pieces of putty, squashed initially between my finger and thumb, to the model until all the areas are covered. This allows you to push down each piece firmly to further flatten it and to get it to adhere better to the surface. By the time this is finished the model will

This rear plate shows some chipping damage applied to the *Zimmerit*. Chipping small areas away along edges or areas of most wear and tear with a scalpel will give a realistic flaking and chipping effect.

be covered in all the right areas but the putty surface will appear very rough. To remove this I take an old blunt scalpel blade and use it like a small trowel. It's essential that you use plenty of water at this stage to avoid getting the putty stuck to the blade and then pulling away from the surface. Applying firm pressure with the blade helps flatten the putty even more against the model. This will produce some overhanging putty that can be scraped or trimmed off with a knife, giving it better adhesion. This approach will work for any area, no

matter how small or large, and by the time it's finished there will be a smooth, thin and uniform layer of putty over all the areas requiring *Zimmerit*. Next the pattern has to be applied before the putty sets hard, otherwise you'll end up with a lot of work trying to remove the hardened putty in order to start again. Fortunately Milliput gives an hour or so of working time before it starts to firm up and quite a bit longer until it has fully set. For flat areas I use the first of my own two *Zimmerit* tools to lightly mark out the ridge pattern. This is just a thin

strip from the side of a CD case that has a series of ridges with spaces that match that needed in this scale. Note that there are different types of ridged patterns on the cases and one other type I've seen, for example, is too large for this. I cut a strip that is just the right width for a single column of ridges and of a height that would cover the height of the slabs on a large vehicle such as a Jagdtiger. This ensures it can cover any vehicle in small scale. Adding a small handle to it will make it easier to control and a piece of plastic tube is good enough for this. Start working from one end of each area and apply lots of water to the surface and tool to make sure it doesn't pull away bits of putty. The ridges on the tool can quite easily trap small pieces of putty which in turn can stick to the surface and pull further bits off. Gently pushing the tool into the putty and pulling away again should result in a nice straight column of ridges. Gradually moving along the part a column width at a time and repeating the procedure until the whole area is covered will result in a very neat pattern of ridges. Photos of real *Zimmerit* show it to be a bit rougher than this so to reproduce this appearance I switch to the other *Zimmerit* tool. This is no more than a chisel-ended strip of plastic of just the right width to create a single *Zimmerit* ridge. Using the ridges just created as a guide I then

go over each one again with this. Rather than pushing at right angles into the surface, an angle of about 45 degrees from under it will push each ridge along a little, giving a more realistic appearance. The other use for this tool is for areas that are too small for the first tool to reach. In these cases the chiselled tool can be used alone to recreate the pattern. Similarly curved surfaces will also require just the use of the chisel. Once the whole model is covered it should be left until the putty is rock hard. Sometimes the surface may appear a bit rough still and a very light sanding can fix this. Don't sand too much though as it will give the tops of the ridges too flat an appearance, which looks unrealistic. One other thing you may wish to do at this point is recreate damaged areas. This is one of the strengths of this approach due to the similarity of the hard putty with real *Zimmerit*. Careful examination of photos shows that *Zimmerit* often chipped away in certain patterns. Along the inner areas of the ridges is one place where it would be weaker and in general areas where the crew would be more likely to knock against it. Just the tip of a scalpel blade is enough to gently prise off flakes of putty. If you have a micro chisel then this is useful for doing this too. Pushing the tip into a ridge and pushing up and away from the model will crack a piece of the putty off in a

realistic fashion. Chipped areas are often seen following along some of the ridges where the *Zimmerit* paste is at its thinnest and weakest.

CASTING YOUR OWN RESIN PARTS

The idea of casting your own resin parts may appear daunting but I hope to show here that casting simple items is really easier than might be thought. In fact fairly complex items can be cast without the need for specialized equipment – it just requires a bit of thought on how they can be split into simpler parts. Professional casting facilities will be able to produce complex multi-part moulds and use expensive pressure equipment. This will force the resin into the smallest of details in the master whilst minimizing the number of air bubbles. The time and money needed to invest in this approach will be out of the reach of the vast majority of modellers, so over the years I've used a very basic setup and some little tricks to give surprisingly good results.

DESIGNING AND SCRATCH-BUILDING A MASTER

I'm going to look at how to create a complex item, in this case a Maybach HL230 engine block as found in the Tiger II tank and its derivatives. Once the master is done I'll look at how to create a mould from it and finally how copies can be cast in resin. Building complex parts like this with a view to casting copies is slightly different from just building a one-off piece. Extra thought needs to go into the design to allow it to be successfully used for creating a mould. You then need to be able to cast copies from it that can be removed easily from that mould. With specialist casting equipment available this type of item could be cast as just a few parts, perhaps even as a single part. In order to home cast it though I designed this item it to be broken down into many smaller pieces – resulting in a small model in its own right. Creating each sub-item in a way that they can be moulded in single-piece, open-sided moulds simplifies things further in terms of the actual mould making and casting. To start I envisage the crude shape of the item, ignoring the smaller details, and imagine how it could be split further into flat-sided parts. For the engine block I concluded that it could be split into three main bits – two side pieces that would join on their flat sides and a top part that would sit directly over them. This would give me the basic shape and from that the next level of detail could be built up. I started by creating the two sides by gluing two sections of thick plastic strip together along their lengths – but

I used two thick pieces of plastic strip for the bulk of the engine block. Gluing these at one end will keep the halves together for the duration of the process and provides a handle to make holding it much easier.

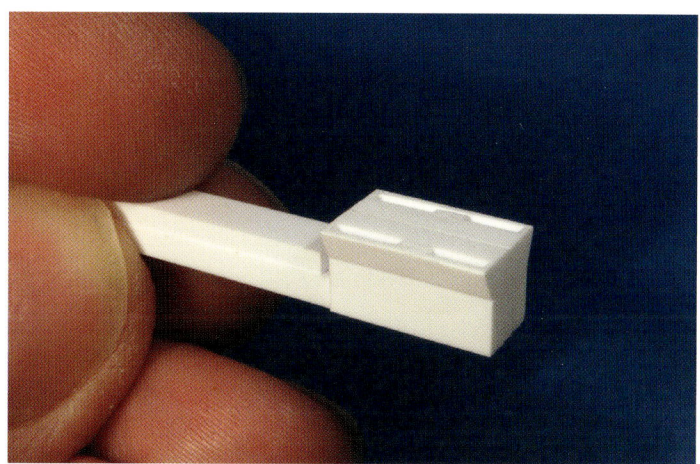

The details are now being built up on the sides. It's important to remember that the parts will need to be removed from moulds. Undercuts are fine as long as they aren't too deep. You should also aim to avoid very thin gaps as the moulding rubber can get stuck in these and tear when removing the part.

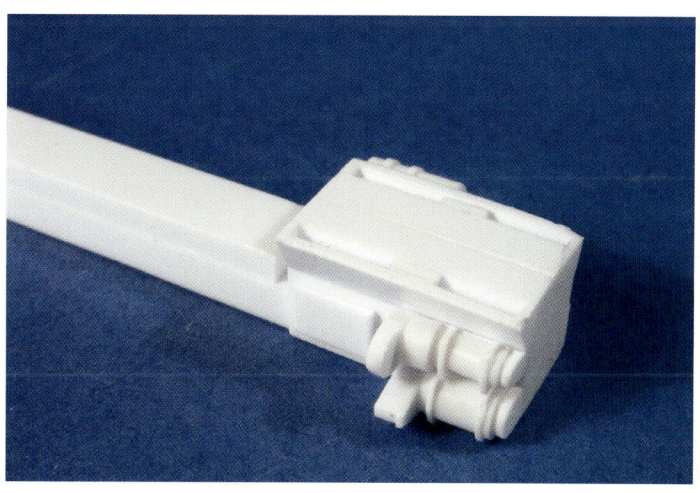

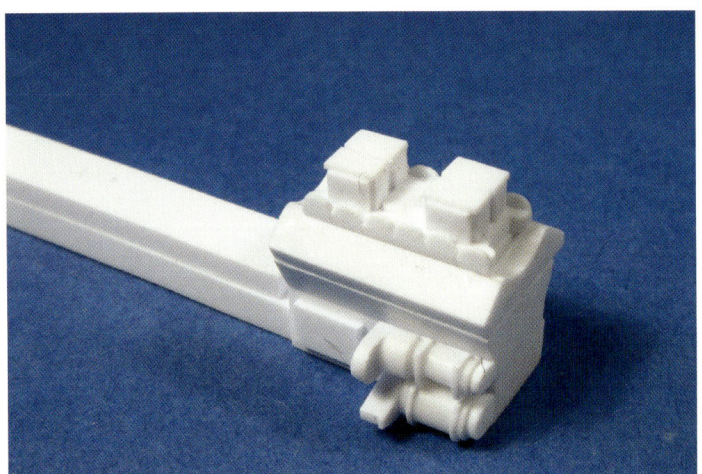

The top section of the engine block is being built up. Again it has a flat underside to make it easier to mould and cast. I've attached it here with a small amount of superglue. This will keep it fixed whilst the rest of the detail is added but will allow it to be separated later when creating the moulds.

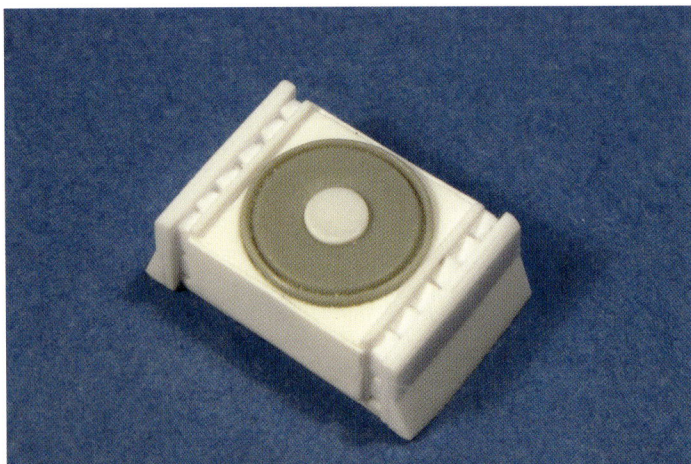

Two air filters sit on the very top of the engine. The central grey part was the only item I sourced from a kit and I cut this from the engine deck insert provided with a Dragon Tiger II.

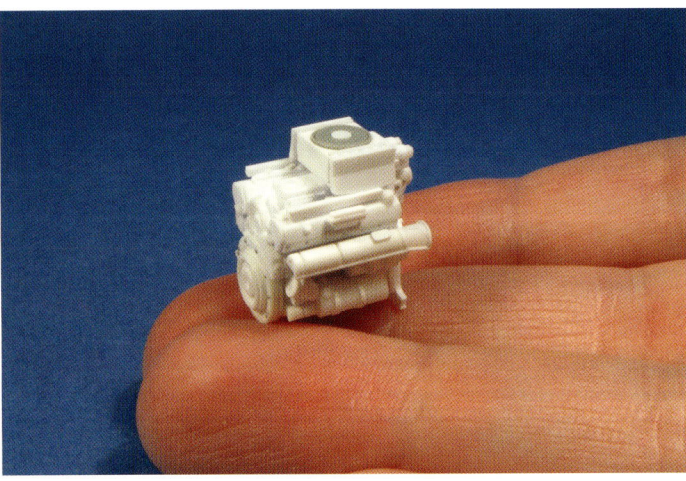

As far as casting will go, the engine block is finished and one of the filters is temporarily sitting on top to give an idea of what the engine will ultimately look like. It requires some plumbing and wiring to be added but these will have to be done after the parts have been cast.

at one end only. Doing this keeps the halves temporarily joined whilst the other details can gradually be built up. The glued half also acts as a handle, making it much easier to hold the piece as it progresses. At the end this can be cut away leaving the unglued halves ready for making the master moulds. It's very important to remember that the part you create will have to be removed from a mould later on.

CREATING A MOULD

In order to prepare a mould I disassembled the engine back into its component parts. These were glued to a sheet of plastic card, allowing a bit of space between each, and some sides were built up around groups of them using plastic strip. The material used to make the moulds is room temperature vulcanizing rubber (RTV). This comes as a thick viscous liquid that sets to form a rubbery solid with the addition of a catalyst. I mix the two in a small metal pan I bought in a kitchenware shop with a small metal spoon. The mixing ratio of the RTV to catalyst is usually given based on weight, and so I measure this out using digital kitchen scales. These are accurate to 1g which is fine for the amounts of RTV I usually mix up. Before discussing the steps of mixing and pouring the RTV I should again remind readers of the importance of safety. RTV and the catalyst in particular are hazardous materials and need to be treated with great care. Always wear gloves when handling them – I use latex gloves as they give adequate protection but are thin enough to allow fine control. You should also wear eye protection. Clear plastic safety specs can be bought cheaply at DIY and hobby shops and provide a perfectly good level of protection for this kind of work. Finally always ensure you have good ventilation as the vapours from the materials are also not too pleasant.

Some of the engine parts have been mounted in a shallow box created from plastic strip and sheet.

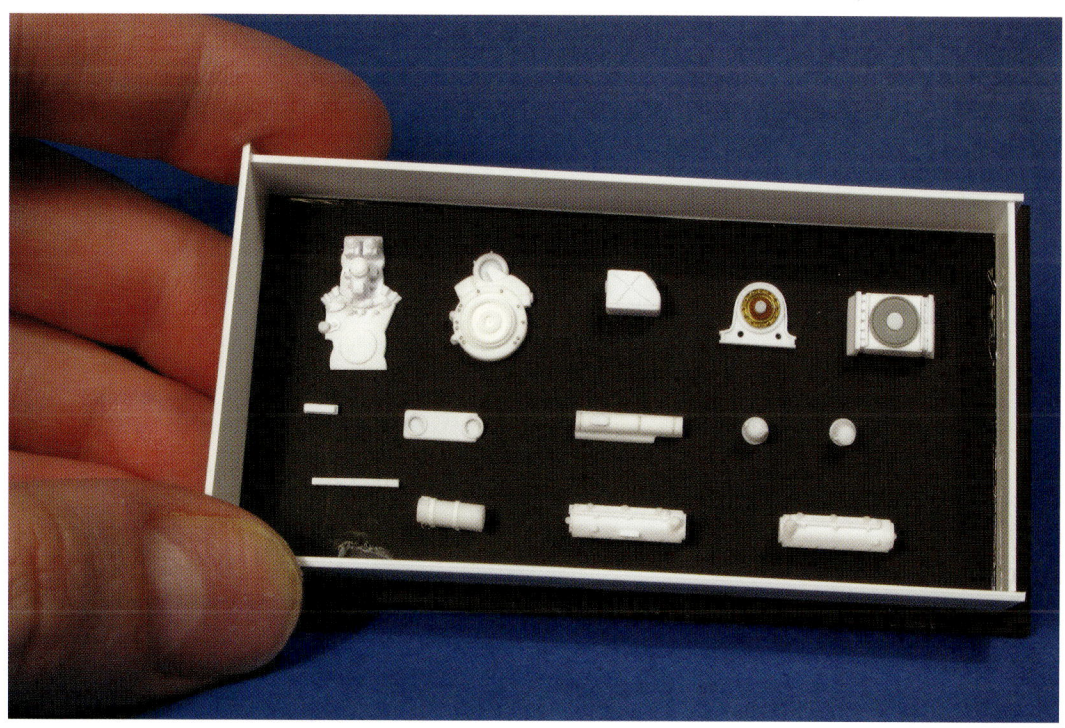

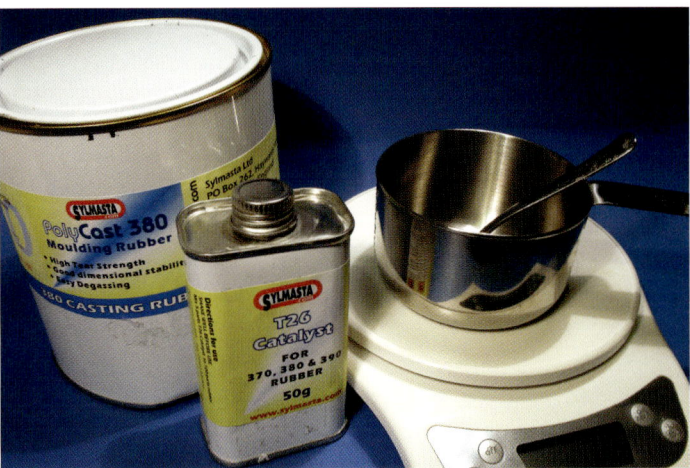

The materials and equipment needed to make the moulds. The large tin contains the RTV. The smaller bottle is the catalyst – a small amount of this will cause the RTV to solidify. Digital scales will allow a precise measurement of both the RTV and the catalyst. I mix it all together in a small metal pan with a metal spoon, both bought from a kitchenware shop. Safety equipment is also important, notably latex gloves and eye protection. Also make sure you work in a well-ventilated area.

The white RTV has been weighed out and the correct amount of dark blue coloured catalyst added based on the amounts recommended in the instructions.

The RTV needs to be thoroughly mixed to a consistent colour. This particular brand gives a working time of about half an hour.

Just pouring the RTV straight into the mould is likely to give rise to air bubbles. An old brush can be used to coat each part with a layer of RTV first to help avoid this.

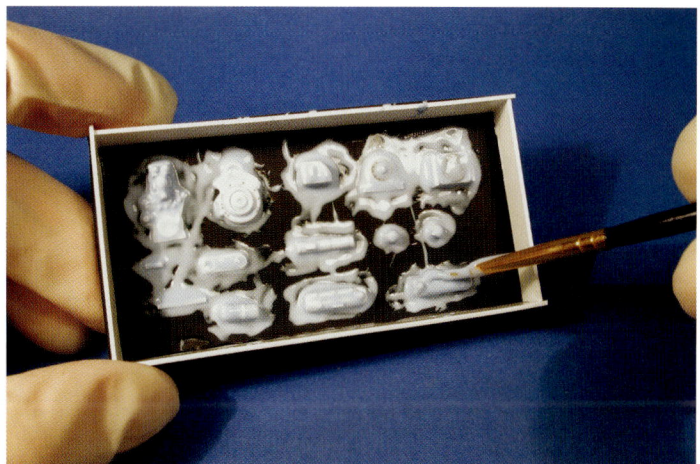

The RTV can now be slowly poured into the mould until it just reaches the top. Leaving it to stand for at least the recommended time will result in a fresh mould that can be carefully popped out of the moulding box.

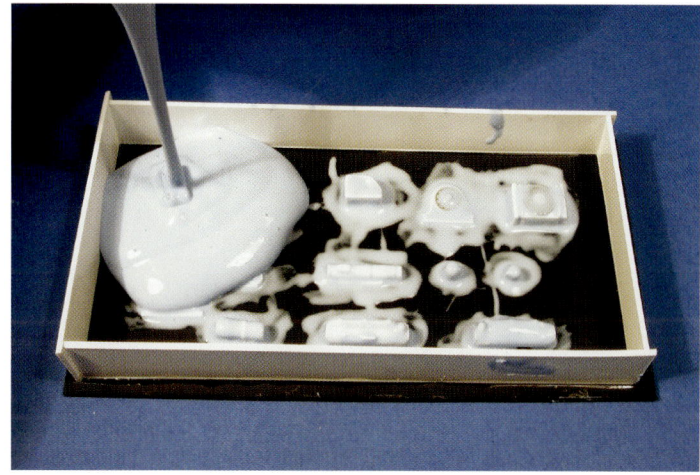

Follow the instructions carefully for mixing the RTV and its catalyst. You need to ensure it is thoroughly mixed with the catalyst but don't be too aggressive when doing this otherwise it will introduce a lot of air bubbles. I've tried a number of brands of RTV of slightly different types over the years and they are all sensitive to the amount of catalyst. Too much and the RTV can start to firm up too soon and become unworkable.

This happened to me once during an early attempt at mould making and the mould was only partly formed. At least I could remove it and start again without ruining the master parts. On another occasion I again added a little too much although not as much as the other time. I managed to pour the RTV but as it set too fast it resulted in air bubbles remaining next to the parts that again resulted in a useless mould. There are techniques

for eliminating bubbles that I discuss a little later that would have helped that time. On the flip side if you use too little catalyst the results can be worse. It may just be a case of having to wait longer for the RTV to solidify but worse still is when it never fully sets. I wouldn't like to try and remove sticky, partly set RTV from lovingly crafted parts. Fortunately I've only added too little on one occasion and it just took a few hours longer than usual to set. As with all aspects of model making – and I've no doubt mentioned this before and will again – practice is the key. Run through the procedure a few times with some unwanted kit parts to get a feel for how to work with the RTV and to pin down the proportions needed. You'll probably also get an idea of the tolerance of the RTV to too little or too much catalyst. Once you feel confident then you can take the step of making moulds from your scratch-built items. It's also wise to then continue using the same brand of RTV if possible. If you switch to another for some reason then I would recommend a few test runs again. RTV varies between brands and even within a given brand there may be different types for different situations. The differences are mostly down to the strength of the hardened rubber and its tolerance to heat and therefore different casting materials. The higher-temperature types are suitable for casting soft metals. Resin doesn't really generate a lot of heat in comparison and lower-temperature RTV can be used. The firmer materials are good for maintaining their shape and structure but the lowered flexibility means that deeper undercuts aren't achievable. I tend to go for a medium level of flexibility as this seems to work the best for resin casting small parts. The RTV

needs stirring well and after doing this I weigh some out directly into the small metal pan. I then reset the scales to zero and add the catalyst, just one drop at a time, until the correct amount has been reached. This should then be mixed reasonably rapidly until it's reached a consistent and streak-free colour. Usually the catalyst is coloured differently from the RTV itself, making it easy to see the point when they are thoroughly mixed. If the RTV is just poured directly into the moulding box it can lead to unwanted air bubbles forming that can ruin the mould. To avoid this, use an old paintbrush to paint the mixed RTV over each part to form a thin layer. This is especially important for small intricately detailed items or those with larger undercuts. When all the parts are covered the RTV can be slowly poured until it just reaches the top of the box. Pouring it in slowly will also reduce the number of air bubbles. As the level rises and covers the parts it will flow into the details and push any air out that wasn't removed when the parts were painted with RTV previously. Now the mould can be left to cure and I always leave this for longer than suggested just to be sure. I invariably mix too much and I have several mould boxes with no parts in them that I pour the excess into. A good use for these will become apparent later when pouring the resin into the moulds.

Doing this also means you can gently check the surface of these to test if the RTV is ready before removing the actual moulds from the boxes. A good rule of thumb to see if the RTV is solid is to press gently onto the surface with the end of a paintbrush handle. The RTV should return to its shape quickly. If a mark is left or it takes longer to return then it's not ready. I also leave the pan and mixing spoon covered in RTV as this can be pulled straight off as a single lump later. It's cleaner than trying to remove the RTV before it's had a chance to set. When you're sure the RTV is ready it's time to remove it from the box. If the box is shallow then gently pulling one edge of the RTV inwards will allow you to get enough of a grip to then pull it away. Take your time doing this to avoid tearing it as it can take a few gentle pulls to remove from any undercuts. If the box is deep or the parts do have particularly deep undercuts then I will cut the box sides away first to enable more room for manoeuvre when attempting to separate the mould. Once removed you are then ready to start casting some copies of the original parts.

CASTING RESIN COPIES

When you've created your RTV mould and allowed it to cure, it's time to start casting some copies of the parts. When first starting out I

I use Polycast resin from Sylmasta (also known as QuickCast) and this cures hard in about three to five minutes. This allows many copies to be made from the same mould in a short space of time. It comes in two large tins and has to be mixed thoroughly in equal proportions.

I mix the resin components in small, soft plastic containers that come as part of Kinder Eggs. These are small chocolate eggs with the container inside holding a small toy. They are a good size for most small items and due to their flexibility any leftover resin can be popped out when set hard.

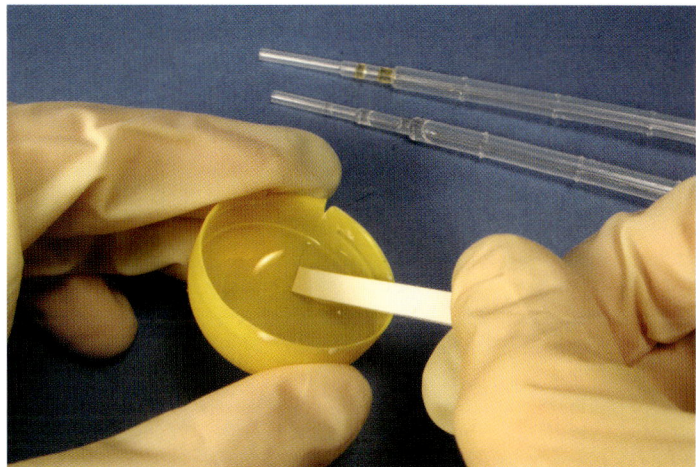

The biggest challenge of home casting is to get the resin completely in the mould without any air bubbles. As I don't have access to vacuum chamber equipment, I buy some cheap brushes and paint the resin into the details. You'll need to disturb the resin, particularly around the smallest details, by jabbing the brush gently against them. This will bring out any air bubbles and they'll rise to the surface. Flexing the mould will also help with this.

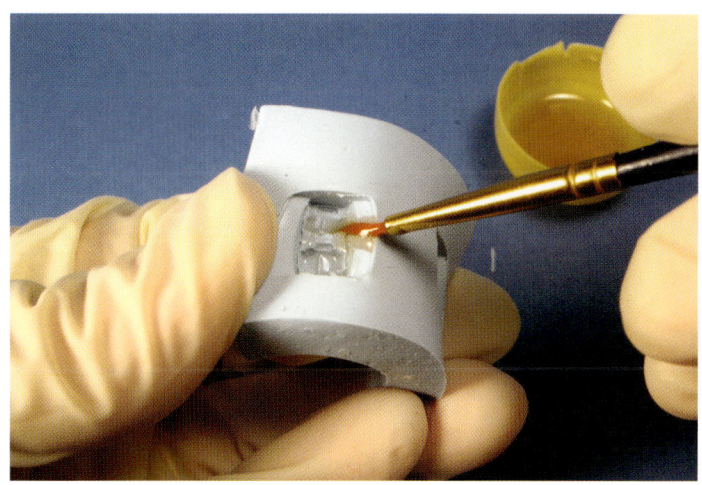

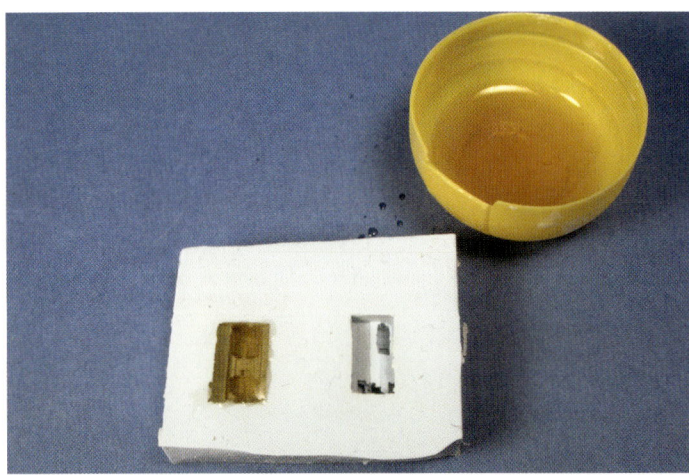

For small items I just load the brush a number of times to fill the mould with resin.

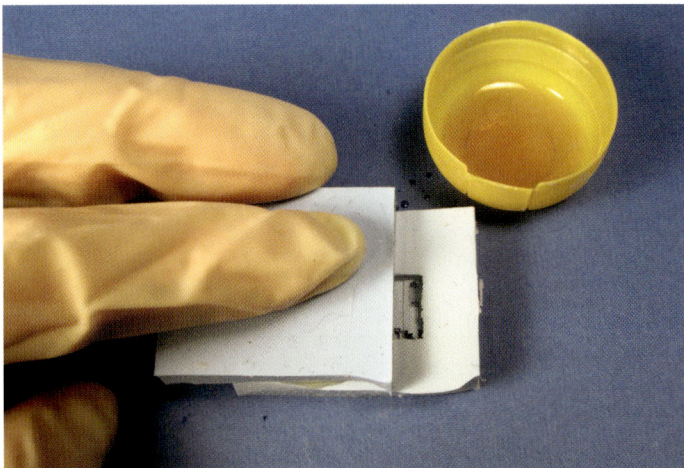

Although I only make one-part moulds, I have a few slabs of RTV that I place over the open mould face once full of resin. This ensures the flat underside remains flat, rather than getting a slight convex shape to it that will require some sanding later.

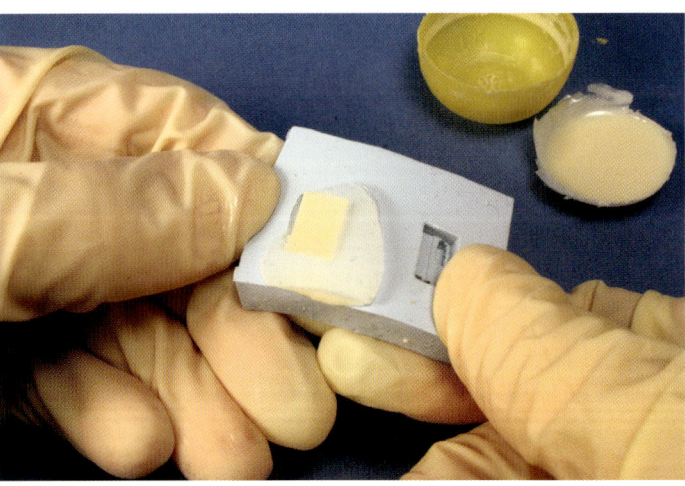

Careful bending and flexing of the mould once the resin is hard will allow you to pop the part out. Note the excess resin that I've removed from the mixing container by just popping it out in one go.

The finished item. This one turned out well but sometimes you'll find one that has a large rogue air bubble or malformed part. Just put this down to experience and try again.

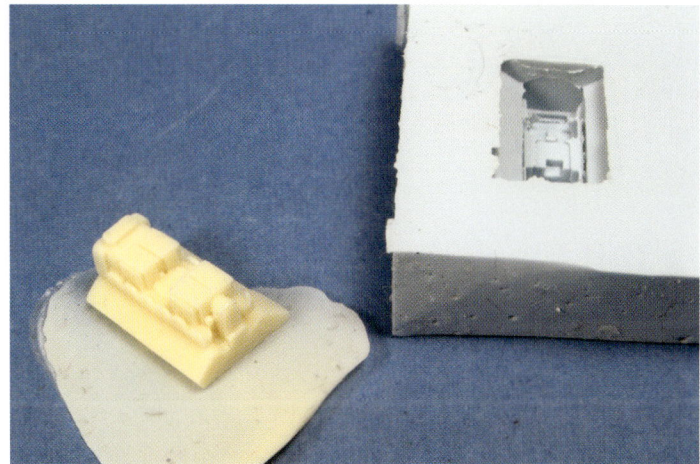

Once copies of each smaller part have been cast and cleaned up they can be assembled into the final piece. Shown here are a couple of engine blocks and transmission assemblies.

This turret is the largest item I've cast so far. Quick Cast is excellent in many respects but its fast curing time can be a disadvantage when working with large volumes of resin.

used silicone mould-release spray for each item as this is intended to make it easier to de-mould parts. It also extends the mould's lifespan by making tears and cuts less likely. However, I've found this unnecessary for small numbers of copies for home casting and I suspect it is aimed more at high-volume commercial work. My preferred resin is QuickCast which comes in two large cans. Both contain a liquid that must be mixed together thoroughly in equal proportions giving a mix that remains workable for just a few minutes. Because of this you have to work quickly and so it's mostly suitable for small items. The largest part I've successfully cast with it so far is a tank turret. If I ever move on to casting hulls I may visit other, longer curing time resins but this has served my needs very well so far. For mixing I use small containers that come with Kinder Eggs. These are children's confectioneries that contain small toys in a chocolate egg. The toys are in a small plastic container that has a soft pliable feel to it. You can easily remove left-over resin by popping it out of the container once it's set hard. The main enemy of successful casting is the air bubble. These can ruin a part by weakening delicate areas and destroying detail. Vacuum chamber equipment can be used to get rid of these but for non-professional use you'll probably need a cheaper alternative as I do.

For this I simply use a cheap throwaway paintbrush. I paint in a layer of resin over all of the details first and work the brush around them to push out any stubborn bubbles. As long as the resin is still in its liquid form these will rise to the top of the mould. I also stretch and flex the mould as I'm dropping the resin in, as this will help it to reach the smaller and more difficult to reach areas. If the part is very small I may just load the brush up one or two more times with resin to completely fill it. For large spaces I then pour the resin slowly in straight from the mixing container. At this point I may jab the brush in around the details again to disturb any lingering bubbles. This should be done quite gently otherwise it can introduce further bubbles into the resin. Although I've only worked with one-piece moulds so far, I have several plain RTV strips and once a mould is full I'll place one of these over the open part to flatten off the top of the resin. This simple step will save you having to sand off excess resin later and gives a perfectly flat underside to the finished parts. Give the resin plenty of time to cure before trying to remove the part from the mould, otherwise it can distort and become unusable. Flexing the mould around the edges will allow you to easily pop the piece out, at which point you should have a bubble-free resin part and a mould ready to make another copy.

BRINGING IT ALL TOGETHER

The methods and techniques I've described in this chapter and the one before can be drawn together to create more complex conversions or even fully scratch-build models. By combining scratch-building techniques with home resin casting you can also make many copies of your painstakingly built master parts.

For major conversion work and scratch-building you really need good scale plans along with as many drawings, sketches and detail photos as you can get your hands on. You may have to scale plans up or more likely down if printed in other scales and this can be done just using a photocopying machine. I have access to a good-quality photocopier at work but often you can find them in print shops or public libraries. My sketches are just quickly done in pencil and sometimes I'll scribble measurements against them. A quick 3D sketch helps me to visualize a finished part and will also aid me in deciding how it might be built. Other useful sources of information are larger-scale kits. Buying one just for reference would be expensive but if you're a member of a local model club you might be able to borrow one from a modeller who builds in such scales (if you ask nicely). A couple of times I've bought one at a much-reduced price in a sale and sold them on once finished to recover at least some of the cost. As

Good scale plans are essential for accurate conversions or scratch-built projects. I also make my own crude pencil sketches of individual parts with the main measurements written in. This is helpful in visualizing what the finished item will look like and will help you decide how it can be made.

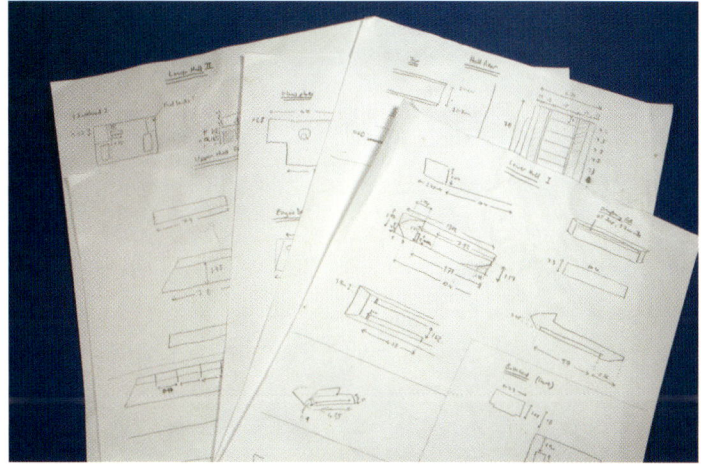

The parts for a scratch-built Grille 17. I had access to a Trumpeter 1/35th-scale model that was useful as a guide. I made sure I compared it to photos and plans of the real vehicle where possible to double-check the accuracy.

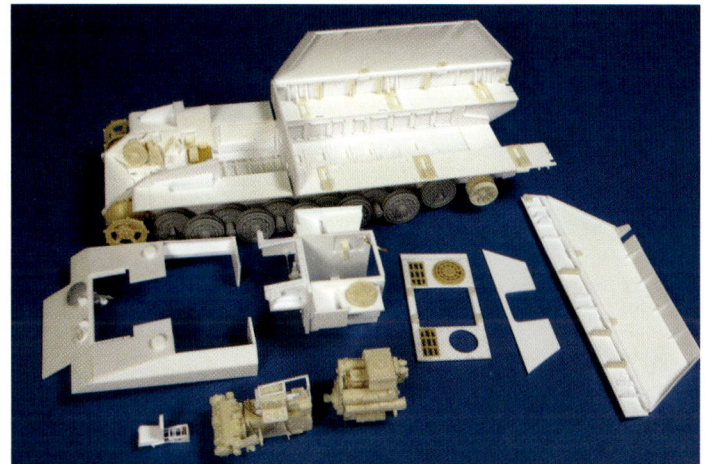

With all the sub-assemblies dry fitted the current progress of the model can clearly be seen. Although the exterior is made of many flat plates, it still required care and planning to get them to all remain perfectly straight and true.

Most of the time has been spent on the interior as this is by far the most intricate part of the model. Although the main items such as engine and transmission have been cast, I added some additional details afterwards. As an example, wiring and tubing can't be cast unless it is lying flat against a surface.

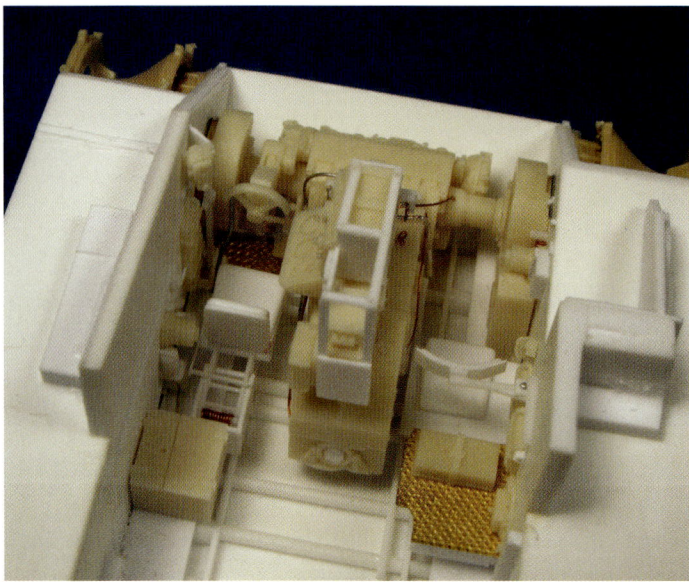

Another close up of the interior. A lot of this will still be visible when the model is finished as I plan to leave the flat plate over the driver's compartment as a separate item.

with most other non-photographic sources you shouldn't assume a larger kit is any more or less accurate than scale plans you might have found. So it's worth investing some time beforehand to determine how accurate a larger model really is

before using it in this way. One approach that some modellers have taken is to generate their own CAD (computer-aided design) drawings and plans. These can be printed off and used as templates from which the real parts will be cut. This

approach is very precise and can lead to some spectacular models. It does require specialized software, however, and additional skills of its own. I haven't taken this approach myself and this is purely because my profession as a software engineer means I spend all my working days writing and working with software. Modelling is a way to get a break from that so the last thing I want to be doing is spending even more time in front of a computer!

The most comprehensive scratch-built project I've completed so far has been a Geschützwagen Tiger Grille 17. There was only one example of the real vehicle built and it was found partly complete at the end of the war. This is still a work in progress that I've been returning to on and off over the last couple of years although the majority of it is now done. My sources for this subject were a little limited due to the fact that only one was ever part built. I had some plans from a *PanzerTracts* book and a number of photos of the captured example at the end of the war. There is also a 1/35th-scale kit available from Trumpeter that I managed to get hold off. The driving compartment interior is now complete and the rear hull interior is mostly finished. I still plan to build the removable gun carriage that would have sat within the cavernous hull whilst the

vehicle was moving. Apart from the wheels that were taken from a Dragon Tiger II it's all scratch-built and it's rare to find a 100 per cent scratch-build as most vehicles share some components in common with others. Modified items from the spares box are often suitable sources for projects like this. The transmission and engine were particularly complex parts and as they were used in other late-war vehicles I decided to cast further resin copies for future projects. When building exterior parts, even flat-sided vehicles that are usually simpler to build can pose some pitfalls. I don't believe in strict rules for modelling, preferring guidelines, but when scratch-building I've always found the following to hold true:

- Always remember to allow for the thickness of the plastic when taking measurements.

- Make test templates for parts first. Don't spend time on a carefully crafted part that doesn't ultimately fit properly.

- Make sure the test templates are the same thickness as the real part will be – if not, for example using paper, then allow for this.

- Repeatedly test fit all the parts to ensure they fit as expected. Do this throughout the whole project.

- Large flat pieces are best made from a couple of thin laminated sheets to give them extra rigidity. This will help prevent them from warping.

- Large structures are best glued with superglue. Never use polystyrene cement as it attacks the plastic and causes shrinkage. This can have a noticeable effect on a superstructure leading to it becoming warped.

Projects like this are naturally very time consuming but also very rewarding. I've still to decide how to paint this model when finished, as the part-built real one appears to have only reached the stage of being painted in red-oxide primer.

PAINTING AND GENERAL FINISHING TECHNIQUES

A well-built model that has had many hours invested in detailing, converting or even scratch-building can be ruined right at the end with a poorly applied paint job. The fear of this has always driven me to keep practising my painting skills as often I have found myself devoting more and more time to the build process. As with any skill, constant practice and experimentation is the best way to improve. When painting a model, I will have either some spare parts or an old built model that I also paint in parallel. This allows each stage to be tested first on this and is especially useful, in fact I would say vital, when experimenting with new methods and techniques. If disaster occurs then the model has not suffered as a consequence.

I cover quite a few techniques in this chapter and although I've presented them in a reasonably logical sequence this can be changed and other techniques mixed in with them. There are no hard and fast rules and I suspect that I've never followed the same order or pattern twice. Finally, you might notice as you read on that I have a relatively small set of finishing products and that certain items keep making an appearance. I try and use as few items as possible to get a job done. This way you can become very proficient in their use, rather than always jumping on the next big thing touted to make your models world class. That's not to say I don't try new techniques and materials out – just that I prefer to find out for myself with a critical approach rather than relying on any buzz or hype.

SOME THOUGHTS ON PAINTING

Before launching into describing my painting techniques I think it's worth mentioning my general views on painting models. Anyone who reads the online modelling forums will have seen debates revolving around the best finishing techniques. These might be how to get precisely accurate colours and whether scale effect (that suggests lightening paint shades for models) is a real phenomenon. In fact the subject of how to get a realistic finish and even what a realistic finish really is seems endless.

ACCURATE COLOURS

There are so many variables that affect the appearance of colour that I don't waste too much time fretting over creating precise colour mixes. The two influences on this are how the weathering and other finishing steps will affect the original base colour and secondly how our perception of that colour varies. For the first issue, the way I weather and shade my models always results in the initial colour changing its shade to some degree. Even if I were painting a factory-fresh vehicle with little if any weathering, I'd still apply some shading steps that would probably darken the finish slightly. So getting a colour spot on right at the start would result in something a little different by the time I'd finished. Because of this I always start with a lighter colour than I intend in the finished model. The other big influence on my choice of colours is that of human perception and environment. Viewing a real vehicle from a distance outside is very different from looking at a scale model indoors at a much closer distance and under artificial lighting. Even its appearance outside will vary

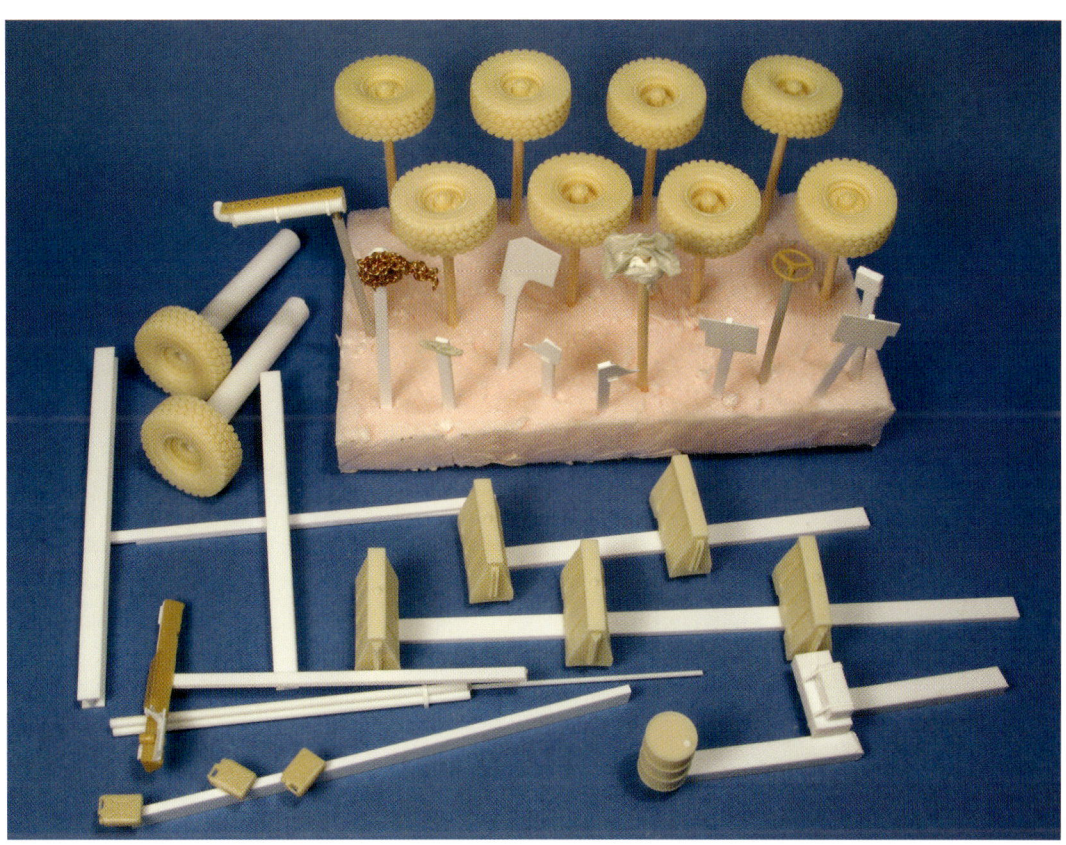

This model has reached the point of applying the first coat of paint. I try and minimize the number of separate parts to avoid unnecessary handling of them once they are painted, although this particular example has quite a lot. The wheels are held with cocktail sticks whilst most of the other items are attached to plastic strips with either Blu-Tack or a tiny blob of superglue to hold them. A piece of polyfoam insulation material is handy for mounting the painted parts whilst they are drying.

depending on the conditions. On a bright and sunny summer's day it will be quite different to that on a dull overcast day during the winter. Put all these factors together and if

you were to use the exact paint used on the original on your model then it would look quite different indeed. Colours appear more muted from further away as light from them diffuses over the distance to your eye. The scale effect attempts to allow for some of these differences and suggests that most colours should be lightened. This will give the impression of an object being further away with a more faded appearance. There are guidelines suggesting that white be added to colours in certain ratios depending on the scale but to be honest I'm

not convinced by this blanket rule approach. For some colours this is clearly unworkable and a good example is bright red where the addition of white would give pink. Therefore different colours need to be treated differently in order to reduce their intensity and simply adding white in each case isn't the answer. My approach is to choose initial colours that already account for this intensity reduction rather than trying to mix my own. Doing this is a matter of experimenting more than anything else and when added to the fact that further weathering and shading will darken the colour, some of the starting colours I use may seem very pale indeed. Another thing to remember is that it's much easier to apply effects that darken a colour whereas making a too dark colour lighter is difficult to say the least.

HIGHLIGHTS, SHADOWS AND CONTRAST

Along with choosing the right colours another challenge is recreating the shaded appearance of a full-size vehicle. As with the perception of colour, this varies depending on conditions but when looking at vehicles outside you'll notice strong shadows in the crevices and panel lines and much lighter highlights. This will be especially marked with a strong overhead sun directly sending most of the light downwards on the subject. A model painted in a single colour without an attempt to reproduce this will look bland and unrealistic in comparison. I've seen beautifully built models that have been painted in a single colour finish with the markings added and then left as finished. To me these still look like models and even a factory-fresh tank will look very different to this with a rich variety of subtle tones and shading. Modellers have an advantage over artists who paint 2D pictures. As the model is a real 3D object we can make use of that to guide us in painting it to look like the real thing and some of the

following examples make good use of that fact. Weathering and shading are two quite different concepts but my approach to painting involves mimicking both of these. As such the steps are intertwined with each other.

PREPARATION AND PLANNING

I always try and envisage how I'll go about painting a model whilst I'm building it. In fact even before I start cutting or gluing parts I will think about how best to construct it so that painting will be as easy as possible. I aim to have assembled as much of the model as possible before painting as I'm not keen on handling and gluing painted parts later on. Having said that, if taken too far it can be difficult getting paint on hard to reach areas. So it's just a bit of a balancing act and trade-off between the two. The decision depends on the subject too. If building a wheeled vehicle I will always leave the wheels separate and similarly I will leave transparent parts separate unless there is no choice – that is if they have to be fitted into a structure such as a cab that will be closed off before painting the exterior. In these cases I resort to careful masking. Tank wheels and tracks are another tricky area. In Chapter 2 I looked at assembling hard plastic tracks where my preferred method is to assemble the track so that it can

be removed from the running gear, with the outer road wheels left separate. Doing so allows the track and outer wheels to all be painted separately, making it much easier to do.

Once the model reaches the painting stage I then look at how I'll paint each part without excessive handling. Larger assemblies such as a turret will usually have a side or area that will be hidden when the model is fully assembled. I will use a length of plastic tube fitted to the underside with Blu-Tack to temporarily hold it. Similarly for a hull, a tube can be inserted down into the turret hole. Smaller parts such as stowage and tools can be a little more difficult to work with. Usually I use lengths of plastic strip and attach the parts with a very small amount of superglue. This will be on an area that won't be visible when the part is finally glued to the model. Make sure you only use enough glue to lightly hold the part for painting as you don't want to be struggling to detach it later. If you follow this method then also ensure you use a type of glue that won't attack the surface of the plastic, so avoid liquid poly and polystyrene cement. Wheels are usually easy to mount and I'll insert wooden cocktail sticks into the hole where the suspension arms will fit. The tapering on cocktail stick ends allows you to trim them at different heights, allowing the diameter to vary to fit almost any wheel. Keeping the fit a little tight will ensure the wheel won't fall off and you can avoid having to use any glue or adhesive to keep it in place. In some instances you may come across wheels that have stub axles rather than holes. For these I turn to plastic tube with a hole that just fits the stub. If none quite fit, then heat stretching a larger diameter section the way you might stretch sprue will give it a taper. This can be cut at a height that will result in the correct diameter that just fits snugly over the axle. In both cases holding a wheel in this way will also make it easier to paint the rubber portion too as you can rotate the wheel whilst holding the brush against it. For tracks that are glued to the sprockets and idlers, I use a similar approach and fit cocktail sticks at either end. With all the sub-assemblies now at the point where they can be held without touching the part itself, you need to decide how they can be stored whilst the paint is drying. Polyfoam is a type of insulation material similar to polystyrene but denser. I use a chunk of this and make small holes that the cocktail strip, plastic rod and strip can be inserted into.

Humbrol satin black has been airbrushed on to act as a pre-shading layer. Any imperfections in the assembly can be more easily spotted at this point, giving you a chance to correct them before proceeding with the next step.

In some kits the parts can have a slightly greasy feel and this is due to the release agents used when moulding them. I've not found this to be a problem on most modern kits but I've come across it on occasion. In the worst cases I clean the whole sprue in warm soapy water and then rinse and dry it off. This isn't usually necessary though and there may just be a bit of oil on the parts from all the handling during construction. If painting with acrylics you need to make sure these areas are completely clean as this type of paint won't adhere properly to the surface otherwise. For enamels their oil-based nature means this isn't so much of a problem and even when I have used acrylics for the main colours I've applied an enamel base or undercoat first. So I start by brushing the parts with a soft wide brush to remove any small bits of debris or dust. Then I'll lightly wash them with a brush dipped in slightly

soapy warm water followed by plain water to make sure there are no soapy areas left on the model. Once this has dried the model is ready for its initial application of paint. I started off brush painting my models but swiftly moved on to using an airbrush as I became increasingly critical of the finishes I was getting. There are no doubt modellers who are skilled at brush painting an entire model but I feel comfortable using an airbrush and it has the benefit of speed for larger areas. I do still brush paint but this is usually for smaller details and figures. I'm going to look next at some of the most common finishes and these include single colours, multi-coloured soft-edged and multi-coloured hard-edged camouflages.

SINGLE-COLOUR FINISHES

The simplest type of finish involves an all over single colour

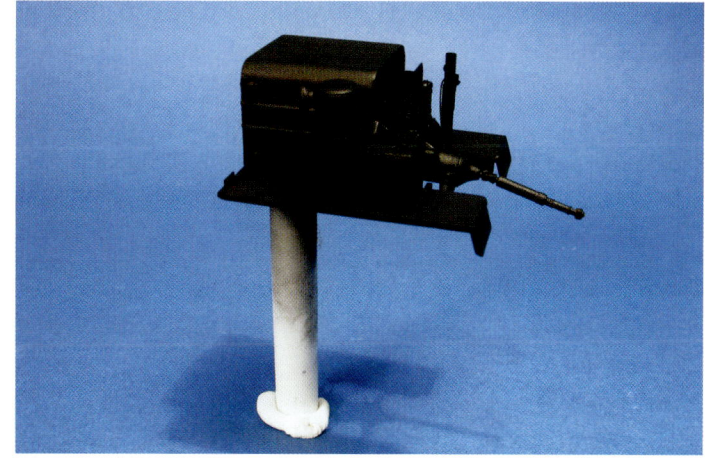

The next colour, green, has been applied in lightly airbrushed layers. Mixing the base colour with a lighter colour and applying this more to the horizontal surfaces will enhance the shading effect. In this case I mixed a light sand colour with the green.

This T-72 hull has had the pre-shading treatment. The colour has gone from a very dark (in fact black) finish to the other extreme of a very light green. Further work will bring this back down to somewhere in between.

and although the easiest to apply it is also the hardest to give an interesting and dynamic appearance too. One long-standing approach to a single colour finish is pre-shading to simulate the effects of strong shadows and highlights. This involves spraying the base colour over a darker undercoat but leaving the darker colour more visible in areas of greater shadow. The choice of initial colour is important as applying a light colour such as pale sand over a much darker colour like black can be difficult. It will require many applications to overcome the stronger colour underneath.

In these cases I might choose a mid-brown base colour and use black for dark greens. Rather than just use matt black, I use Humbrol Satin Black as a pre-shading base. Satin and gloss black appear darker than the matt equivalent and I want as dark an effect as possible to start in order to give a strong shadowing effect. The base colour can then be sprayed over the top of this in light layers, allowing it to build up more on the highlights and horizontal areas that would catch more light. When doing this keep the mix dilute to give a smooth transition between the colours. Doing this also allows the effect to be gradually built up with finer control. For larger featureless areas, concentrating the colour within the centre will give a nicely artistic effect and add to the perception of depth but this can be easily overdone and look unrealistic. For areas like this I apply a degree of panel shading but subtly mottle the top colour over the pre-shaded layer too. This gives an effect more akin to texture mapping as seen on computer graphics and breaks the

monotony of a single colour up in a more realistic and interesting fashion. The process can be repeated more than once and also with increasingly lighter versions of the original colour. When reaching lighter shades the effect should be kept more on the top surfaces to give the impression of stronger overhead light. When mixing the lighter shades avoid using pure white. This will lighten the shade but the strength and vibrancy of

the colour can easily be reduced too much. For green I use a light sand colour which gives a degree of warmth to the mix.

HARD-EDGED CAMOUFLAGE SCHEMES

Some finishes require two or more camouflage colours that have hard-edged demarcation lines between them. Perhaps they were brush painted on the real vehicle,

When painting a multi-coloured camouflage, it's best to paint the whole vehicle in the lightest colour first. Then mask the areas that are to remain this colour with thin, rolled-up pieces of Blu-Tack.

Some areas will be a little trickier to mask due to their shape or small size. The gun barrel on this Tiger II was masked by applying a long strip of Blu-Tack along the top and then forming a wavy, curved shape using a wooden cocktail stick.

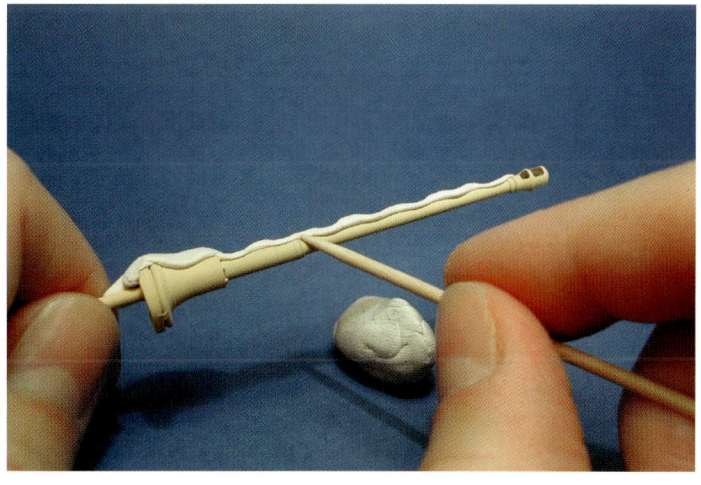

After applying the next lightest colour, in this case light green, again mask off the areas that are to remain this colour.

The procedure of masking and painting needs to be repeated until all the colours have been applied. Some finishes may require four or even more repeats of this.

When the final colour is dry you can peel away all the Blu-Tack to reveal the final effect. Any imperfections can be fixed with a small brush.

or stencils and other forms of masking were used when the colours were sprayed on. If you brush paint your models then this type of finish won't really pose much of a problem. Lightly painting the outlines of the pattern with a small brush first will guide you when filling the blocks of colour in. For those using an airbrush masking will be required in order to achieve the effect. My own preference for this is to use a variant of Blu-Tack putty. It has enough adhesion to stick to the model securely whilst painting but can be removed quite easily without causing damage. Another similar medium is Silly Putty sold in toyshops. Masking tape can also be used but I find it harder to cut to the right shape and it doesn't sit well over more complex shapes and curves. The flexibility of putty allows it to conform easily to the most complex of surfaces and it can be repositioned and reshaped as much as needed until it gives the correct pattern. Start by painting the lightest colour first and then gradually work up towards the darker ones, as it's harder to get good coverage of lighter colours over dark. Once the base colour is fully dry I start to mask the areas that are to remain in this colour. For broader areas I roll thin

This sWS has received two coats of Humbrol Matt Cream (103) for the base colour.

sausage-shaped pieces of Blu-Tack between my thumb and finger. These are curved to the desired shape and gently pushed onto the model along the borders. A cocktail stick with the ends rounded off is useful to have at hand as you can use this to further shape the edges of the putty. In order to get a sharp and clean edge you need to keep the putty flat with the surface but don't push it down too firmly as it will end up difficult to remove later. The next colour can now be sprayed over the top. Keep the mix thin and don't apply too much otherwise it will build up against the edges of the putty leaving a ridge at the boundary. This procedure will need to be repeated as many times as necessary until all of the colours have been applied. When the final application of paint is dry the moment of truth arrives and you can remove the layers of Blu-Tack to reveal a clean

hard-edged camouflage underneath. A fresh blob of Blu-Tack is useful as dabbing it over the masked areas will help pull them away more easily. At this point you can touch up and fix any minor issues such as overspray or missed areas with a small brush. The camouflage colours will more than likely look garish at this point and before doing anything else I very lightly overspray a heavily thinned layer of the lightest colour over the whole model. This helps blend and tie the colours together and give a more in-scale appearance to it.

SOFT-EDGED CAMOUFLAGE SCHEMES

Unlike hard-edged camouflage finishes, soft-edged finishes are ideally suited for an airbrush. Small mottled patches of colour can be replicated in other ways, however, and I've seen good results using both pastels sealed with a coat of

As I wasn't representing a specific vehicle I applied the camouflage by freehand with no guides. I started with the light green first, keeping in mind that there were to be areas of red-brown to be filled in next. When working freehand I slowly build the camouflage shapes up using a very thin mix of paint at a low pressure.

A more realistic effect can be achieved by toning the camouflage colours down. A very dilute overspray of the base colour is ideal for this.

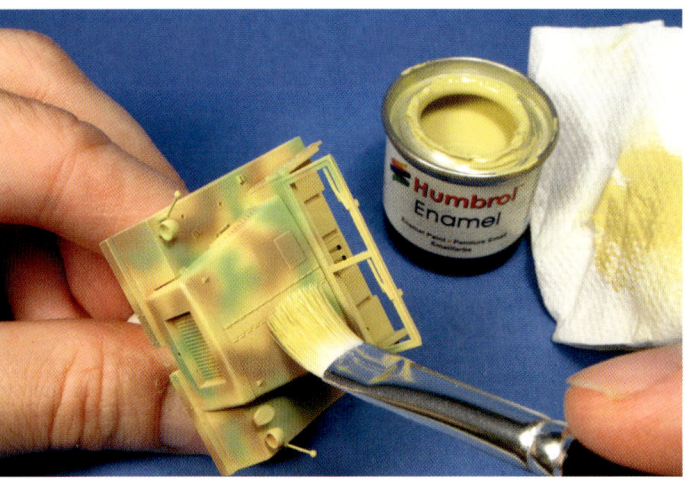

Some subtle dry brushing can tie the main colours together and add a bit of extra highlight to the finish.

varnish and dry brushed patches of colour. For small mottled patterns it can be difficult getting a fine enough spray pattern to satisfactorily apply them. In these cases a small brush to dry brush them on can be a lot easier to control. For larger patterns of colour an airbrush is in my opinion definitely the best way. If you are trying to replicate very specific shapes rather than just some random mottled effect then the key to getting a good pattern is to mark it out on the model first. A dilute mix of the colour you plan to spray can be applied with a small brush, just inside the area where the boundaries lie. Sometimes I won't be modelling a specific vehicle in which case I may just have an approximate idea of the patterns I want and I'll then spray them free hand with no guides. I'd recommend marking the

patterns if this is something you've not done much of before but after some practice you won't need to do this. When spraying the pattern aim for a dilute paint to thinners mix, thinner than the main base colour. Using a reduced pressure with this will allow for the greatest degree of control and finesse as you gradually build the colour pattern and strength up. With paint this thin it's important to keep the pressure low to prevent it flooding the surface and causing paint runs. I don't set to a precise pressure setting but just use experience and intuition to adjust it each time. As when working with hard-edged patterns, start with the lightest colour first and work through to the darkest colour last. Similarly, I will apply a light overspray of the base colour to tone this harshness of the colours. You can vary the amount you do

this depending on a number of factors. If you want to portray a sun-faded effect then you might want to go a bit heavier with it. Take care not to get carried away though and end up removing most of the strength of the colours unintentionally. To prevent this I paint a spare part in the main colours and frequently compare this with the model as I start to tone the colours down. Replacing this with a light dry brushing of the same base colour can achieve similar results and in some cases I actually do both.

APPLYING MARKINGS

Real vehicle markings are usually painted on and suffer the same weathering effects as the rest of the paintwork. Some advise that you should apply markings immediately after the base colours

Some of the options available for adding markings to your model include waterslide decals, dry transfers and painting them yourself. The latter two are my preferred methods. A couple of examples of aftermarket dry transfers are on the left of the picture. For the painted option you can use hand-cut masks for the simpler cases or hand paint them if you feel you have a steady enough hand. An example of an etched-brass stencil set from Stencilit is shown on the right of the picture. They are available for a number of subjects.

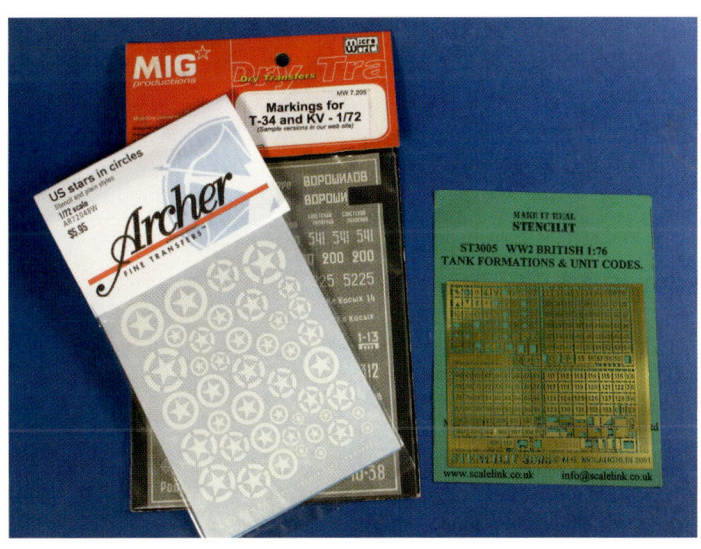

This Israeli Merkava IV features white markings created from stencils from the Stencilit range.

so that they receive the same degree of weathering as the rest of the model. This is good general advice, but sometimes I will run through a few of the initial weathering stages so as not to tone the markings down too much.

There are several choices available for adding markings to your model. Kits mostly provide these as waterslide decals, which consist of the markings printed on a clear background held to a backing paper by water-soluble adhesive. Soaking these in water

for a short time will soften the adhesive, allowing them to slide off the backing paper onto the model. There are many companies that sell similar aftermarket decals to further expand the choice of finishes. Another aftermarket option is that of dry transfers. These are rubbed down over the surface of the model and don't require any water. A third option is to paint them yourself, either freehand or with the help of masking or stencils. A company called Stencilit make some etched-brass stencils that include 1/72nd-scale subjects. Each of these options has its strengths and drawbacks. Some waterslide decals

have a thick carrier film and lack a true painted-on look. Air bubbles can also get trapped under a decal and give a silvering appearance through the transparent areas of film. There are a few ways to minimize these issues and the silvering problem can be improved by applying the markings to a smooth glossy surface. A smooth matt finish will have a rougher surface than an equivalent glossy one and this makes the problem of tiny trapped air pockets far greater. There are commercial decal-setting solutions that soften the decal, allowing it to adhere and conform better to irregular surfaces. This will also reduce the problem of

The markings here are a mix of the kit's waterslide decals, some Archer dry transfers and hand painted ones. I applied them over a coat of Klear acrylic varnish, followed by another coat to seal them afterwards.

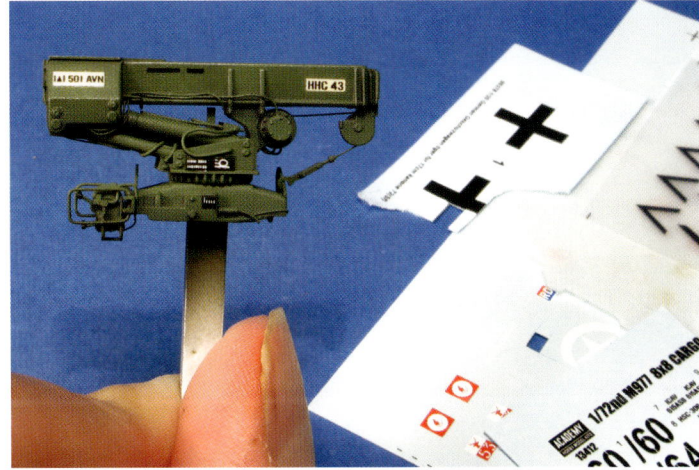

silvering. My own preference though is to avoid wet decals whenever possible and use dry transfers instead. I'm a big fan of these as I've found it much easier to avoid some of the issues mentioned above and as they are extremely thin they have a more painted appearance when applied. It won't always be possible to find dry transfer options and in those cases I look for the availability of stencils. I have several generic stencils sets from Stencilit that cover German, Russian, US and British World War II and modern Israeli subjects. These can be attached to the model using small strips of masking tape around the edges and the paint applied with the airbrush set to a low pressure. There are two things to watch out for here: firstly make sure the masking tape covers a reasonable area around the stencil to avoid any overspray onto the rest of the model. Secondly make sure

the stencil lies flat against the surface to avoid paint getting under the stencil.

CREATING PAINT CHIPS AND SCRATCHES

Small paint chips and scratches will build up on a vehicle over time, especially in harsh climates. The crew will cause some of this by climbing on and around the vehicle, particularly around the crew hatches and upper surfaces. Showing this type of weathering is popular amongst modellers and if done well adds much to make a finish appear realistic. It's also very easily overdone, however, so the phrase 'less is more' is especially relevant here.

A quick and easy way to replicate these types of effects is to use a small torn-off strip of artificial sponge. On multi-coloured camouflages, gently dabbing the base colour over the other

camouflage colours is a good way to show them wearing away to reveal the base colour again. This can be further enhanced by showing weathering further down the layers of paint. This might be to a primer layer or even just bare metal. This should be even more restrained as each new layer of paint that is revealed usually exhibits less of a worn effect. This can clearly be seen on modern construction equipment. A deep paint chip that runs through multiple layers of colour tends to show the smallest surface area at the innermost layer. For small-scale models I usually just go for the darker colour of bare metal and a good representation of this is Vallejo SS Camo Black (122). It's a very dark colour that is almost black but with a slight hue of reddish-purple. Pure black can be a bit harsh and this particular colour is a good alternative. For this type of weathering acrylics seem better at giving the finest possible

A quick and easy way to represent worn-off paint is to use a small piece of torn sponge. To show the topmost layers of paint wearing away this can be dipped in the base colour and gently dabbed along raised areas, edges and other points of high wear.

Vallejo acrylic SS Camo Black (122) is a good choice to represent scratches down to the bare metal. This effect should be less pronounced than the scratches to the base colour previously shown.

scrapes and scratches, although I do apply it with enamels depending on the colours involved.

BREAKING UP UNIFORM SURFACES

Once the overall colours and markings have been applied to a model, further shading and weathering can be started. This is my favourite part of finishing as it is where the model really comes to life. There are many weathering techniques that I've used over the years and I've probably never weathered two models in exactly the same way. I used to think that the best way to improve and gain consistent results was to formulate precise recipes for weathering. Up to a point I still follow this, but rigidly following it will probably lead to lots of models that all look quite similar. Rearranging the steps, or reapplying the same ones more than once will give a more unique finish and may even lead to new ideas and better end results. My advice is to avoid falling into a rut following identical routines for each model. One thing I do always start with is to give the model an overall coat of Klear acrylic varnish. As I described in the section on markings, this helps protect both them and the main colours when carrying out further weathering steps. It also has a nice shine to it that provides a good foundation for many of the following weathering steps. Applying a single thin covering results in a satin finish and I find this to be better than a fully gloss finish. For the next step I apply an overall dilute wash to the model. If applied over a completely matt surface there is the chance of staining this permanently whereas a shinier surface allows you to correct areas and work further with it, even when touch dry, for a short time. The wash itself has three

effects. Firstly it adds depth to the finish by running into and around the smaller details. Secondly it breaks up the monotony of the surface. Finally it tones down the shininess of the Klear underneath. I use Humbrol paints for the washes and to dilute them I always use Humbrol's own brand of thinners. I've experimented with other types of thinners, including the household DIY variety but have achieved the most satisfactory results with the own brand. Some

of the household types are quite aggressive whilst Humbrol thinners are much milder in comparison and of course are designed to work with the same brand paint from the outset. Its mild nature also means there is less chance of disturbing any areas of underlying paint that didn't get a proper coverage of Klear. The strength of the wash can of course vary considerably. If made very dilute it becomes more of a tinted glaze or to use a proper modelling term a 'filter'.

Klear acrylic floor varnish is great for getting a tough, shiny finish and due to its thin, water-like consistency is easy to airbrush. It helps protect the markings and main colours from the next stages of shading and weathering. If applied lightly it gives more of a satin finish which I find ideal for applying washes and other weathering steps to.

More often than not I apply an overall wash to the model. This will add further contrast to the surface. It's particularly useful for single-colour finishes as they have the potential to appear dull and boring otherwise. The wash can be further worked over almost immediately either with additional applications or just neat thinners.

This turret is also getting an overall wash of dark green. The base colours were created with a number of very light green shades. A medium strength wash will bring that back down to a more realistic appearance.

A brush dipped in thinners can be used to selectively remove the wash from small areas to achieve stronger contrast in the finish.

Localized applications of very dilute paint mixes are useful for adding variation to surfaces. These are often called glazes or filters and can be applied to the whole model to change its hue. Here some green is being applied to a few single planks of wood on this cargo bed.

Filters add depth to a finish and my own use of these is more for changing the shades and hints of finishes where I'm not completely happy with them. Often many of them in many different shades are successively applied. At the other extreme are strong washes that will have a pronounced effect on the appearance of the model. I mix my washes probably somewhere in the middle, maybe more towards the stronger end. I apply them with a broad, flat brush to sections of the model at a time and as soon as dry I'll rework the area a little. To do this I have another clean brush dipped in thinners to hand. Applying a thin layer of neat thinners over the area just treated will allow you to further blend the wash and vary the effect in selected places. Again I don't use hard and fast rules and may return to an area more than once.

STRENGTHENING THE SHADOWS

An extremely important part of finishing a model is to enhance the shading and shadows. Although a model is a 3D object, and will by definition create its own highlights and shadows, these will not appear strong enough to be comparable with viewing a real vehicle outside. Some of the previous steps such as pre-shading and the application of washes will themselves add a degree of contrast to the model. For the smaller details and stronger shadows this still isn't quite enough. A good method for getting a strong shadow effect is a 'pin-wash'. These are localized washes around details and along panel lines, usually involving a more concentrated mix to achieve stronger shadow effect. A very dark colour is best for these, such as a dark brown or even black. Adding some oil paint to the mix will

extend the drying time, allowing you to work with the effect further once on the model. This is where a prior application of Klear varnish is important as it prevents the wash from staining the surface and allows you to correct any mistakes. I start working along the model in small areas, firstly applying some thinner over the area. Before this evaporates I'll lightly dab the pin-wash around the detail and the thinner will help draw the colour around it. Keep another small brush to hand as you can use this to remove any excess and correct the application if there is too much wash. It's time consuming working along every detail but after this step you'll really notice an improvement in the finish. On some occasions I apply one or more additional applications to strengthen the effect and in some cases after other weathering effects have been applied. For the very

A pin-wash is being applied to the details. Paint thinners have been applied to the area first to help the wash flow around the details. You should aim to keep this type of wash as tight as possible around the details to give the impression of shadow, rather than just a painted line.

deepest details I'll finish off with pure black wash, giving a gradation of shadowing effects.

REALISTIC DUST EFFECTS

Getting a dusty finish that is both realistic and visually pleasing can be difficult. Simply applying dust-coloured pigments or paint to a model can cause it to look flat and reduce the impact of the detail. You also need to think logically about the areas where dust would be more likely to settle. Most of the time you can see it on horizontal or near-horizontal surfaces as gravity will prevent accumulations on vertical and steeply sloped surfaces. In the same way that paint chips and scratches will normally be found near moving parts and areas of crew activity, removal of settled dust will occur in a similar way. Whether you use pigment powders/pastels or paints is a matter of personal taste. Pigments can be more easily removed if you want to modify the effect or are unhappy with it. On the flip side it means they don't have as much staying power on the model over long periods of time. Fixing them with matt varnish may seem to offer a solution but I find that doing so further flattens the finish and reduces the impact of the pigments. I prefer paint as you can

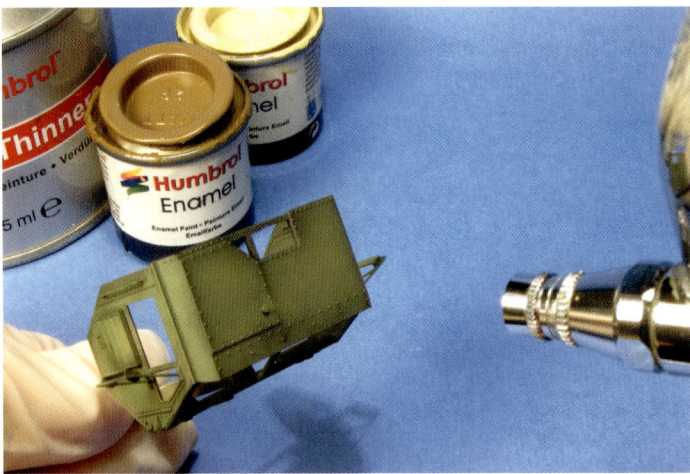

To represent dusty surfaces, I spray a very thin and dilute paint mix over the horizontal surfaces of the model.

I immediately load a broad paintbrush with thinners and 'paint' over the whole area. This will appear to remove the dust colour but as the part dries it will return. More of it will remain in the crevices and around details with raised details remaining in the base colour.

Dry brushing the base colour over the model provides a way to reduce the strength of the dust effect.

In some cases you'll need to mask off areas such as those that are vertical to prevent the paint from accidentally spraying onto them. Some low-tack masking tape is fine for this.

Once the colour has been sprayed on the mask can be removed and thinners used to blend the effect in.

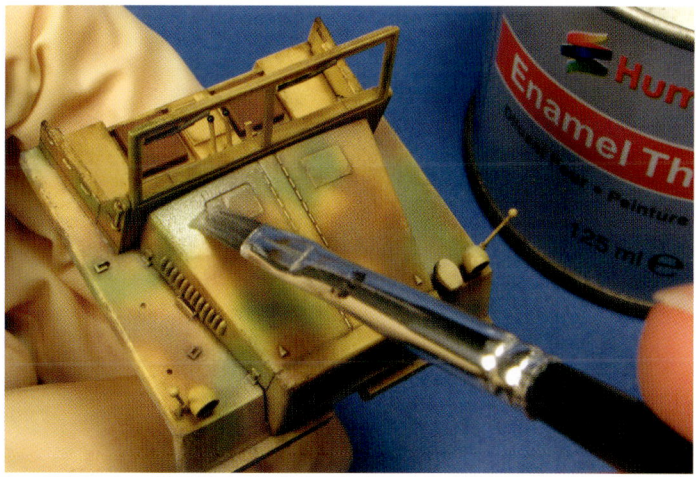

The completed dusty finish. At this stage I reapply some of the previous shading techniques such as pin-washes to bring strength and depth back to the details.

still work with it for a while once applied, and in the long run it has more staying power. I often apply further weathering or shading steps afterwards too and this would disrupt a pigment application.

I usually start by masking off any surfaces that I want to keep free of the dust effect. Typically this will be vertical parts of the model. I then mix up a dilute dust mix – Humbrol Pale Stone (121) is a good starting point – and to this I may add other colours depending on the shade I'm looking for. Using a low-pressure setting for the airbrush and a dilute mix allows for the greatest control over the application and I'll gradually build up the effect. Again think about how the dust would settle. On a horizontal surface you'll usually see more of a build-up of dust at the point where it meets a vertical surface so I concentrate the mix more at these types of areas. One thing to watch out for is too heavy a build-up of the effect. It can be easy to get carried away with this as it can appear quite subtle, so make sure you stop occasionally and compare the look of the area you're working on with the rest of the model. When the effect looks good then it's time to stop. I then take a clean brush dipped in thinners and paint a thin application of this over the area. This will temporarily darken the paint and it will appear that the dust effect has been lost, but it will return shortly. This has the effect of changing the way it blends with the colour of the model and I may repeat it more times. It gives a more random effect to the blending rather than the perfectly feathered effect the airbrush alone will typically give. It can also be a way of getting a streakier appearance. When the whole model is complete it needs plenty of time to dry before carrying on with any other weathering or shading. I previously described the pin-wash method of accentuating shadows and details and I may apply pin-washes multiple times at different stages to ensure the shadow effects remain strong. This is especially relevant when creating dusty effects, otherwise the contrast will slowly be lost as the dust effect is built up. Deposits of dust will be affected by light and shadow just as any other area and applying a pin-wash back over will restore this effect.

RUST

The addition of small rust deposits is a great way to add some variety to the finish of a model. Applying rusty effects should be treated with the same caution as adding paint chips and scratches. Firstly it can easily be overdone

Small localized rust effects can be represented by painting them in with dilute orange enamel paint, but don't overdo this effect. It's wise to study photos of the real vehicle if possible when trying to reproduce effects like this. The rust I'm applying to this truck is based on photos of the real thing. They showed the lower part of the frame as being more prone to rusting.

To add depth to the rusty areas paint a smaller patch of a darker shade in the centre of the orange areas. Burnt umber oil paint mixed with brown enamel gives a good colour for this.

The field-applied appliqué armour shown here was first painted black followed by an overspray of a dark rusty brown colour. Successive orange and brown washes were applied next. Finally small amounts of orange and black pigment powders were dabbed onto small selective areas.

and secondly you need to research your subject enough to determine which parts would rust and which wouldn't. I'm going to look here at just creating small areas of rust. Other methods can be employed to create larger areas that might be found on abandoned or burnt-out vehicles, including the 'hairspray technique' described in the next chapter. For small spots of rust I start by dotting on small amounts of dilute orange enamel. This needs to be dilute otherwise it just looks like what it is – orange paint. It gives a more subtle effect and you can go over the area to strengthen it as needed. Next I take a darker rust colour, again an enamel such as Humbrol Rust (113), but with a small amount of burnt umber oil paint added. The oil paint serves two purposes. It gives a more vibrant colour and

secondly it gives more time to work with the effect. This is especially useful for vertical rust spots that can often be seen to streak downwards. Once applied a small damp brush can be used to drag the spots down, creating a feathered streaking effect.

For larger areas of rusted metal such as a metal sheet or exhaust I'll start by painting it black first. After this a patchy spray of orange-brown will start to create a more rust-like finish. The next step is to apply a series of rust-coloured washes. For some of these I'll dab the wash on rather than apply it with smooth brush strokes and this will give a more random and natural appearance. Finally I'll take some pigment powders, orange initially and then black, and selectively blend these into the finish.

OIL AND FUEL STAINS

Another little trick that can add to the realism of a finish is the addition of fuel spills, oil and grease stains. These can often be seen around fuel tanks, drums and wheel hubs. Commercial mixes are available to represent these but it's quite easy to mix your own. Mixing enamel thinners, black enamel paint, gloss varnish enamel paint and burnt umber oil paint will give a very realistic concoction that can then be applied as needed. The gloss varnish is an important ingredient and gives a realistic translucent appearance to the end result. Being gloss it retains an oily look even when dry. I don't keep precise ratios of these and prefer to just mix a bit of each together and try it on an old model or scrap plastic first until I'm happy with the result.

The materials needed to create your own oil and fuel mix – enamel thinners, black enamel paint, gloss varnish and burnt umber oil paint. The gloss varnish will give it a nice shiny, translucent appearance.

Apply the mix around fuel tank filler caps, but as with rust effects keep this to a minimum.

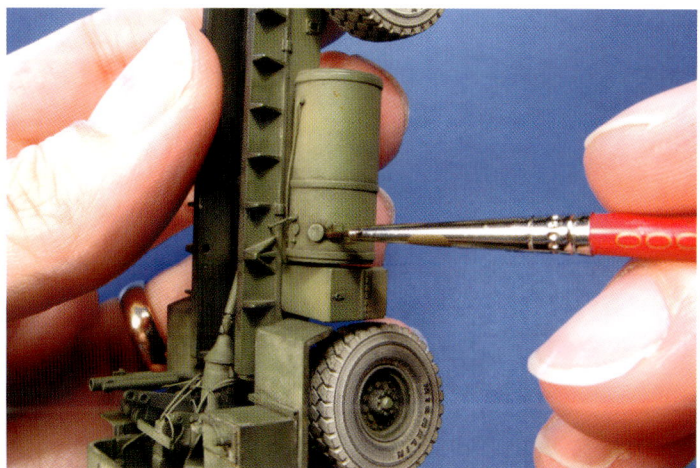

Envisage how gravity will draw any oil spills down vertical sides. Try to work from photos of the real thing if you can to get a good idea of how it should look.

Spills and leaks that form over horizontal or near horizontal surfaces will tend to pool more. Apply the mix in a more dotted pattern in these cases to build up a cloud like effect. If there are vertical sides nearby then the effect can be made even more eye-catching by dragging it down these in streaks.

WEATHERING WHEELS AND TYRES

Earlier I mentioned that I leave wheels separate from the model until after it has been painted. This makes painting and weathering them a simpler task, especially for those with tyres or rubber rims rather than all-metal types. If the tyres are moulded as a single piece to the wheel there are a number of approaches you can take to painting them. Wheel masks for individual vehicles are available in 1/35th scale but currently I've only seen one example of this for a small-scale model. You could make your own wheel masks of course but I use a couple of other methods instead, depending on the size of the wheel. For those that are small, such as return rollers or small road wheels, I just hand paint them with a fine brush and a thinner than usual mix of paint. Panzer IV wheels would be a good example here and by keeping the paint thin it will be easier to keep greater control of it. If you've fitted the wheels into cocktail sticks or plastic rod, then slowly rotating them whilst lightly holding the brush up to the rim should make free hand painting this way much easier. For larger wheels such as those on a truck or perhaps a halftrack it's sometimes possible to fill the tyre colour in by airbrushing it. Any overspray onto the hub can be wiped away immediately with thinners. Another approach I often use is to paint the whole wheel in the tyre colour first and then paint the hub in afterwards and in fact I've always done it this way when pre-shading a model with black. So what colour is best for tyres? I've read and heard many times that you shouldn't use pure black as real tyres don't look like this. I think the second part of the statement is true but I always use black for a number of reasons. The first time I painted a tyre I lightened the black with a tiny bit of white and the resulting dark grey just didn't look right. It had a cold, bluish tint that didn't have a convincing rubber look to it. Adding some dark brown rather than white was better, giving a warmer feel to the appearance. If you take a look at real tyres that have seen any use you'll notice that they get an ingrained brownish look to them and seem to almost soak up any dust. Having found that a very dark brown colour looked better, I noticed the following day a small area I'd missed. Unfortunately I couldn't

To get a realistic rubber effect, paint the tyre area black and then lightly spray a dilute brown mix over it. I use Humbrol Dark Earth (29) for this. Any overspray on the hub can be removed with a small brush dipped in neat thinners.

Don't overdo the application of the brown otherwise you'll have to clean it off and start again. Comparing tyres before and after shows the difference in appearance.

In order to get a more filthy and dusty appearance, flood the tyre with pure thinners once the earth colour is touch dry. This will appear to darken the colour and the tyre will look black again. When it dries the dust effect will return.

The thinners will evaporate more quickly if you blow air through an airbrush over the wheel. This will also push the thinners around, forcing them into the tyre tread and other details.

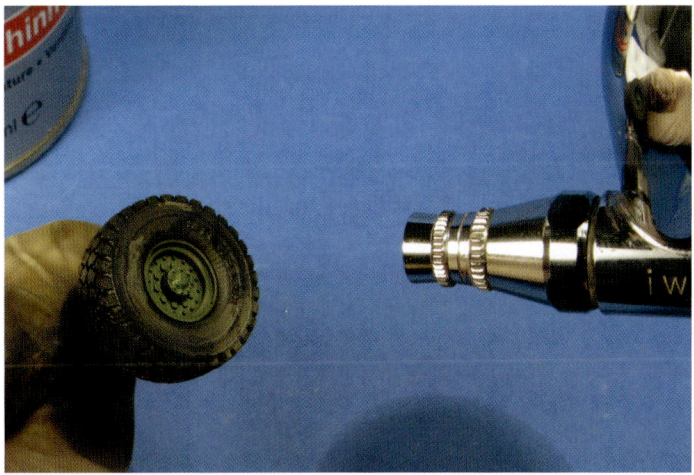

To recreate dust wearing off the tyre tread, dry brush black enamel over it. Doing this to other raised areas will also add additional definition.

The finished wheel. Note how the dust lies more heavily around the details. The effect is less uniform than you would get by simply airbrushing a dust colour on.

recreate the exact mix of black to brown. From then I just started using black and let the subsequent weathering steps tone it down.

With a tyre now painted black you can look to reducing the harshness of the colour and representing dust, dried mud and other weathering effects. The type of weathering you'll want to apply to the wheel will of course depend on the context of where the vehicle is. If you're modelling a vehicle in

a hot, dry climate such as the desert then you'll probably want to achieve a dusty and sandy appearance. For damper climates a mix of wet and dry mud might be more appropriate. At the other extreme are winter conditions with snow, ice and muddy sludge. Another option is to just go for a minimum of weathering, perhaps on a newly manufactured vehicle. I start by airbrushing a dilute dark brown colour over the black,

usually Humbrol Dark Earth (29). A bit of overspray onto the hub isn't a problem and in fact when wiped away with a clean brush and thinners will add to the grimy appearance of the wheel as a whole. For a fairly new vehicle with little or no dirt then you could stop at this point. To get a more dusty appearance I flood the whole tyre area with pure thinners. You need to do this as soon as the paint is touch dry otherwise it will

Another dusty wheel, this time from a Famo halftrack, shown fitted to the model.

be hard to get the desired effect. The next step is to blow air through your airbrush to speed the evaporation of the thinners. This will also force the thinners into the cracks and details, taking more of the brown paint with it. As the thinners evaporate the dusty colour will quickly return and this time it will have a more random appearance, being stronger around the details and tyre tread crevices. Pigments diluted with thinners will achieve a similar effect, but I prefer the better adhesion of paint. Sometimes I'll augment the effect with a final light spray of Dark

Earth but without a final treatment with thinners. Although Dark Earth is a good choice for a generally dusty appearance you may want to vary the shade, perhaps by adding some sand or other pale colours. For a vehicle serving in desert environments I'll add some Pale Stone to the mix for a lighter finish.

On a real vehicle the raised areas of the tyre tread will make contact with the ground as the vehicle runs over it and so the dust will tend to wear away on these parts. This isn't always the case and I've seen photos of vehicles with the tread faces in a pale dust colour and the crevices darker. I imagine this depends on the amount of dust and perhaps other factors, but having the dust

settle in the cracks and crevices looks appealing to my eye and appears to be just as common. To increase the contrast between the high and low points of the tyre apply a light dry brushing with black over the tread and other highlights. You should now have a nice dusty-looking tyre and you can repeat the steps to build this effect up more if you want to.

PAINTING AND WEATHERING TRACKS

Tank tracks can be weathered in a similar way to tyres regarding the build-up of dust and dry mud. Their appearance will vary considerably not only between different vehicles but also depending on the environment. Something you should avoid are overly rusty tracks. A layer of bright rust deposited over them might look attractive but it isn't very realistic. There are times when this sort of appearance might be appropriate – for example a burnt-out vehicle where fresh rust will quickly form. An abandoned vehicle that has been left to the mercy of the weather for some time will also start to show rusting around the tracks. As time moves on this lighter-coloured fresh rust will start to darken. In the case of an operational vehicle there will quite possibly be small amounts of rust to be found but I keep this to a minimum. I treat bright metallic areas in the same way; restricting them to those areas that repeatedly get worn down as the vehicle moves. All-silver tracks never look realistic and only areas that are constantly being scraped or rubbed against other parts will

have a bright metallic appearance. I discussed several methods for assembling tracks earlier but when painting them I always start with pure black. This is similar to the approach I took with painting tyres and is really just an example of the pre-shading method. I also follow the initial steps I took with tyres by airbrushing dilute Humbrol Dark Earth over this, flooding thinners on top and then drying it off with the airbrush. This gives the tracks a grimy look and tones down the pure black base colour. I'll often give a second or third run through with this approach, varying the dirt shades each time. When the track is dry I'll look to simulating the shiny metallic areas, for example where the raised parts on the outside of the track come into contact with the ground. Other common areas of wear are the guide teeth as these will rub against the wheels and idler and areas in contact with the sprockets.

These effects can be added using metallic paint applied with a small or medium flat brush. For the track exterior I use a kind of dry brushing but with a little more paint (perhaps damp-brushing would be an appropriate term). Smaller details such as the guide teeth faces are best done with a smaller brush. Although the road wheels will also rub against the track, it is often less pronounced as the soft rubber of the tyres doesn't have such an abrasive effect. To simulate the wear from tyres I run some black pigments along the inner face of the track up against the guide teeth at the point where the wheels will come into contact with it. At this point I will stop weathering the separate tracks and continue with any further steps once they've been attached to the model. To simulate mud flicked up onto the vehicle by the tracks, take a mud-coloured paint and load some on a wide brush. Flicking the

The tracks have received a pre-shading covering of matt black paint.

Humbrol Dark Earth is being patchily sprayed over the black.

As soon as it's dry, I flood thinners over the track to loosen the newly dried paint.

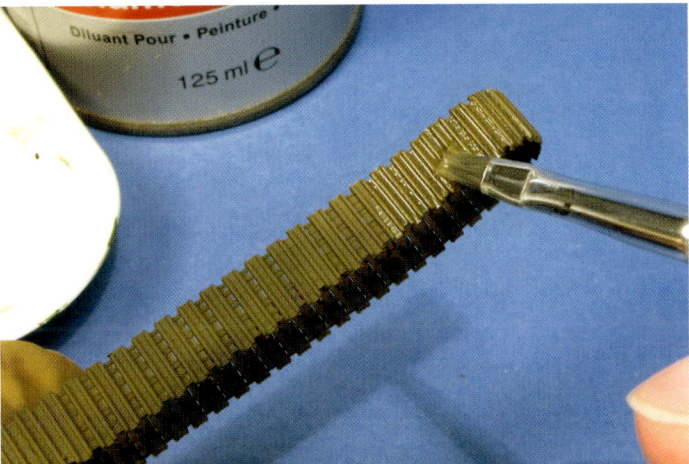

Blasting the track with air will dry the thinners and force the paint into all the nooks and crannies. It may seem that applying a brown wash would have the same effect, but I've found it appears better when done this way. Not all the brown paint lifts away, leaving it more opaque in areas and this is something a simple wash wouldn't achieve.

I lightly dry brush metallic silver over the highlights on the outer track face. The guide teeth also receive the same treatment. Apply this sparingly as too much bright metal looks unrealistic.

I run some black pigment in strips along where the wheels sit. This will give the impression of mud and dust being removed by the friction of the wheels as the vehicle moves.

After the tracks have been attached to the model you can simulate mud being thrown up onto the vehicle by flicking muddy coloured paint onto it. I work over a sheet of white paper as I can test and clearly see the effect just before applying it to the model more easily.

brush against a cocktail stick will spatter small deposits of paint against the sides of the vehicle in the way real mud gets thrown up. Working over a light-coloured surface such as plain white paper will enable you to quickly test out the method and see the results more clearly before applying it to the model. Do think carefully about where the mud would most likely fall and the angle at which this would occur. Mimicking this will give the most realistic results.

REPRESENTING DUSTY WINDSCREENS

Under dusty conditions a windscreen (or windshield) will soon gather a fine layer of dust. Windscreen wipers will wipe away much of this and the common design of two pivoted wiper blades in front of the driver and passenger will create a characteristic double

crescent pattern of clean glass. There's some debate about whether the effect is as strong as modellers sometimes represent it as being or not. As usual for these types of discussion I try and find photos showing the effect. There's no doubt that it can be seen, particularly in dusty environments and if well done the effect really enhances the look of a model.

Masking the areas to be kept clean and using paint for the dusty areas is the obvious approach to this. Dust-coloured paint might seem ideal but unless the application is extremely fine then it can look too heavy and opaque. Matt varnish is a better alternative as it results in a more natural and realistic translucent effect. Using masking tape is one way to mask the areas but I make thin plastic templates instead. Doing it this way makes it easier to cut out the right shapes, allowing them to be

sanded. It's also easier to position them due to the lack of adhesive. In the example illustrated here I used the thick kit windscreen as a template to create a thinner acetate replacement. I then temporarily fitted the kit item to the model whilst painting it – the visible area of this ends up painted over. I built a small frame around the piece using plastic strip to hold it steady and then created the two plastic masks for the areas I wanted to mask off. The painted areas of the kit windscreen can then be used as a guide to help position the masks. To make the masks I cut a circular piece from plastic sheet using a compass cutter. Sometimes I'll make the disc by temporarily supergluing a piece of plastic sheet to the end of plastic tube of the correct diameter and cutting and trimming around this. This can then be carefully removed from the tube. I open up a smaller hole

The key to getting a realistic dusty windscreen is to get a sharp, precise boundary between the clean and dirty areas. I make a small holder to keep the windscreen and masking parts together at the right position. Shown here is the original kit windscreen that I constructed the holder and masking parts around.

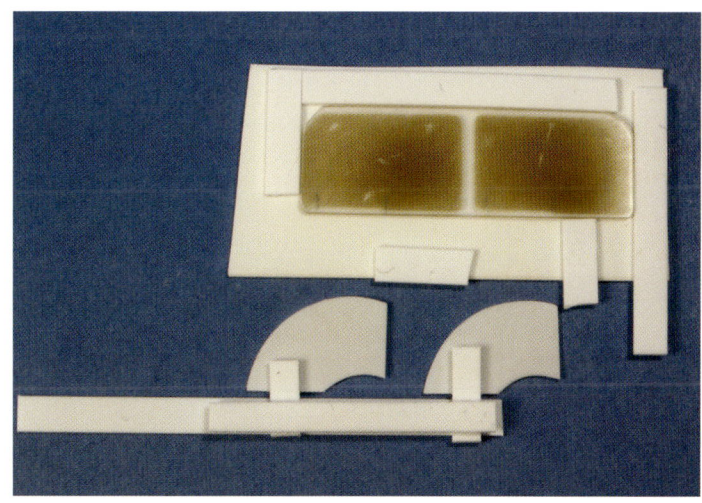

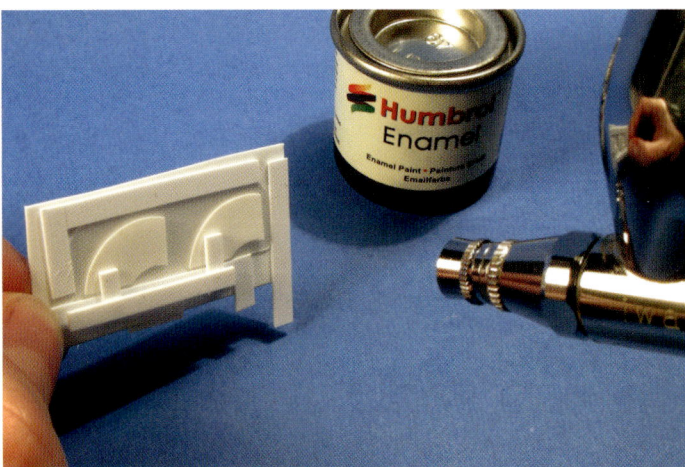

Lightly spray matt varnish over the windscreen, keeping the application consistent and evenly applied.

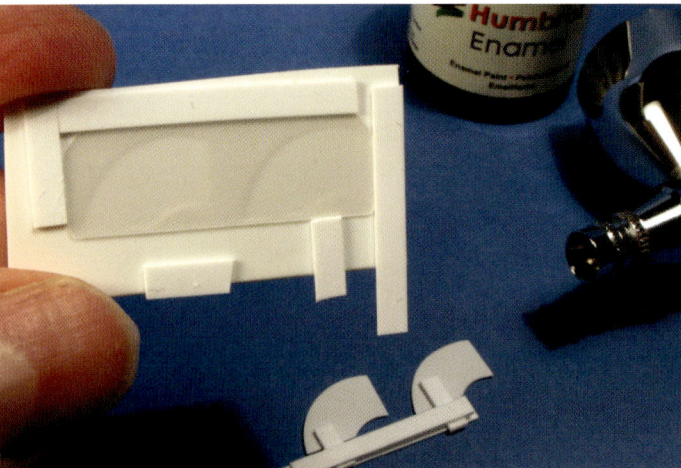

Removing the masking reveals the unpainted areas.

The windscreen fitted to the finished model shows the results to good effect.

in the centre with a round needle file and then cut at the appropriate angles to give the two mask pieces. I fix these to the holding frame and insert the replacement acetate in. It's now ready to be sprayed so I mix up some dilute matt varnish and very lightly and smoothly apply it over the whole windscreen. Tilt the piece towards the light so that you can see its reflective surface initially. This will then show you how much varnish is being applied as the reflections start to disappear as more varnish is added. Once dry you can simply remove the windscreen and it's ready to be attached to the model.

DOES A FINISHED MODEL NEED VARNISHING?

It can be tempting to apply a blanket coat of matt varnish to a nearly finished model but I steer away from doing this. The main reason is that it gives the model a flat, dead-looking finish that to my eye just doesn't look right. Studying photos of military vehicles or seeing them in the flesh shows varying degrees of sheen to most finishes. Occasionally they can be almost glossy, but usually it will be somewhere between the slightest of sheens and a satin finish. Weathering effects such as dry mud and dust will cause a finish to take on a more matt appearance overall, but unaffected areas or those where it has rubbed off will regain their former look. Edges will get buffed more than flat areas and gun barrels often have a noticeable sheen to them. As I always apply a thin covering of Klear varnish this gives the model a satin finish to start with. Subsequent weathering steps will gradually reduce this down with the effect being more pronounced in some areas than others. This gives a realistic and pleasing richness to the appearance that would be lost with complete matting down. It may be the case that the model retains too much shine and in these cases I selectively spray dilute matt varnish onto the model to reduce this to a degree. This would tend to be on lower areas that exhibit more dust and dry mud.

PAINTING FIGURES

Figure painting is really an art form in itself and over the years I've seen some incredibly well-painted figures at model shows. I spent a long time focussing just on building and painting vehicles and avoiding figures as they present some unique painting challenges of their own. I was concerned that including unrealistic figures would spoil a good model and this fear meant it took some time to start seriously considering the addition

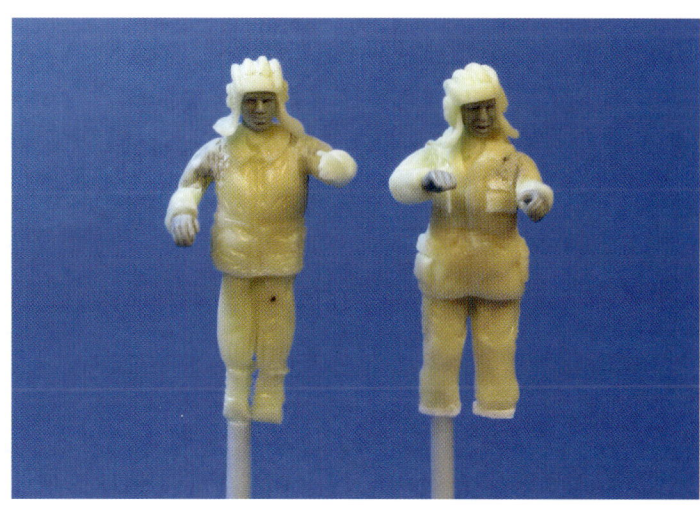

To make handling figures easier whilst painting, I mount them by drilling out a small hole underneath and inserting plastic rod.

The figures have received a black enamel base coat followed by the uniform colour, a brown shade airbrushed on. The black serves as both primer and a pre-shading layer. Another lightened application of the uniform colour can be applied at an angle downwards to give the impression of overhead light. This is a simple attempt at reproducing the so-called Zenithal Lighting approach to figure painting.

A slightly darker version of the uniform colour is used as a pin-wash around the creases and wrinkles in the uniform.

A pure black pin-wash has been applied to the sharper creases and folds. This is further blended in with a fine brush dampened with thinners.

I use a couple of brush-painted applications of Humbrol Flesh (61) for the base skin colour. A dilute brick red mix is good for adding areas of mid-tone shadow and this is also blended in with another clean brush.

Thinned burnt umber oil paint is added around the areas of darkest shadow. These will be the eye sockets, sides and underside of the nose and the mouth.

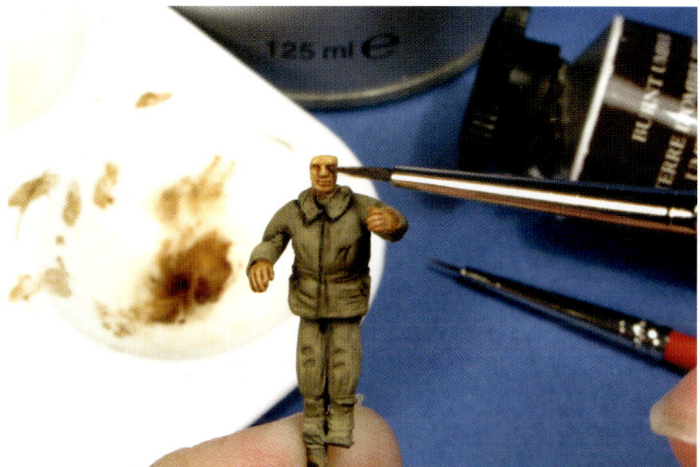

Highlights are added in using the original flesh colour mixed with a small amount of white and an even smaller amount of red. The precise mix of this should be varied depending on the context of the figure. A desert tank crew would require more of a sun-tanned appearance so I might not add as much white. Adding some red gives a more vibrant, fleshy pinkness to the skin. Apply this to the highlights such as the cheekbones, forehead and top of the nose.

The finished figures with the helmets and other remaining details painted in. Some modellers paint the eyes in but I've not been happy with the results I've achieved when doing this. At this scale the eyes would be difficult to see anyway so I rely on adding strong shadow instead.

of crew to my models. The small size of the subject matter and trying to shade a 1/72nd-scale face and perhaps even paint things such as eyes and uniform details is very difficult. I'm definitely no great figure painter but I've reached the stage where I'm happy to include crew figures with most of my models now. In fact I will always do this if I can find some suitable ones of good enough

quality. One clear thing I learned early on is that the sharper and more realistic the detail, the easier it is to paint the figure. The small size of the subject means that shading and highlighting are of paramount importance and strong, crisp detail will make it much easier to achieve a good result. Some of the best figures I've seen are resin ones and often they have sharper detail than injection-moulded counterparts. The injection-moulded Preiser range from Germany has some good figures available and there is a small but growing range of excellent figures included in some of the Dragon kits. The Dragon ones are smaller versions of their highly regarded

1/35th-scale counterparts and feature separate legs, arms and heads along with fantastic detail. There are also many white metal figures to be found and some of these are very good too. I prefer resin and plastic over these as white metal has a slightly coarse texture to it that can become more apparent when painted, but this doesn't prevent me from using them occasionally. At this point I should also note that although I don't mix 1/76th-scale vehicles with my 1/72nd-scale collection, I do mix figures. As they are very small and the size of humans varies it's not such a problem. There are also differences between manufacturers. By this I mean that sometimes you can find a 1/76th-scale figure from one company that is actually slightly larger than a 1/72nd-scale figure from another. Because of this I always consider figures in both scales and take them on a case-by-case basis.

The following painting example uses some resin modern Russian tankers from Armory of the Ukraine. They have a single colour uniform and are a good type of figure to start with. For these I removed the heads and hollowed out the helmets to take replacements from a Dragon set. The Dragon heads are amongst the best I've seen and this makes painting the faces much easier. Replacing parts in this way also gives some individuality to your figures.

Right: These winter tank crew figures are based on white metal figures from the AB wargaming range. I replaced the heads with one from a Warriors figure set and a couple from MIG Productions as the detail on these were better. It also allowed me to pose the heads at different angles.

Below: The coarseness of the white metal shows up slightly when looking at the finished figures but under normal viewing isn't noticeable. Note the shine on the middle figure's helmet, achieved by painting it with Klear varnish before shading and weathering.

PAINTING – ADVANCED FINISHING EFFECTS

This chapter looks at some painting techniques to achieve finishes involving more than just the application of base colours, shading and weathering. A popular example of a more complex finish is a winter whitewash. Another involves the opposite extremes of weather – the desert. Desert conditions can prove harsh and even the hardiest of paint finishes will take a battering from the heat and effects of sand scouring its surface. Large amounts of dust can also build up on vehicles and then selectively wear away. I'll look at both these extremes and the different ways of achieving them.

APPLYING A WHITEWASH FINISH

In order to blend in with a snowy landscape, military vehicle crews may apply a temporary white finish to the vehicle. This can be done in a number of ways but one of the most common is to apply either a complete or a patchy covering of temporary whitewash paint. This allows the white to be removed once winter has passed in order to return to the original colours. The temporary nature of the paint means that it can easily scratch and rub away. This can make for a very appealing finish to a model and the scope of this is large, ranging from a completely white vehicle as if just freshly painted to a very weather-beaten and worn appearance. For me the heavily weathered look is the most interesting. I'm sure many modellers find weathering enjoyable but it can easily be overdone with too many paint chips and scratches all over the place. A scruffy

whitewash finish provides scope for the modeller to really go to town and there are many photos of extremely worn finishes on real vehicles. As you might expect, there are many methods for achieving this kind of look. I'll briefly mention a few of them but focus on my favourite technique. These methods aren't all mutually exclusive however and I do mix some of them together.

HAND PAINTED

A simple method of producing a whitewash finish is to apply the white colour in patches and then dry brush the base colour back over it to simulate the more worn-down areas. The white itself can be brush painted and kept thin to give a slightly transparent effect to it. This can mimic well the real method of crudely applying thinned white paint to the vehicle but carries the risk of a creating a model that just looks badly painted. Applying the white by

airbrush gives a more appealing finish and this can still be done to leave patchy areas. Heavily worn effects should be concentrated around areas that are used the most often by the crew such as the hatches and the edges and areas around them. Also any other access hatches, on the engine deck for example. Further refinements to this can be added in with a fine brush – again using the base colour – to reproduce areas where the paint has completely come away.

REMOVAL WITH THINNERS

Rather than adding areas of the base colour back in by repainting them on top of the white, you can wear the white away to uncover the areas underneath. This mimics the real ordering of events more closely and I used this method for a number of years. It's best to use different types of paint for the base colour and the white or to apply an intermediate varnish layer. I've followed this approach by giving an application of Klear acrylic varnish to protect the enamel colours underneath. Spraying a thin layer of patchy white over this, again using enamel paint, and then waiting until it is just touch dry gives the opportunity to start wearing it off. A stumpy cut-down paintbrush is dipped in enamel thinners and scrubbed over the areas of whitewash you want to remove. This can give some nice effects but if the white is too thick or had too long to dry fully it can be difficult to remove. Applying more thinners and pressure to the brush may end up pulling the base colours away too, although the Klear layer helps to avoid this up to a point.

MASKING METHODS

There are several related methods that involve pre-masking the base colours before the white is applied. One of these methods uses Maskol, a liquid latex substance that can be stippled over the base colour with a teased-out piece of a scouring pad – the kind used in kitchens for cleaning away thick dirt from pots and pans. This gives a nicely random, fine pattern and once the white has been airbrushed on top it can be removed to leave areas of base colour showing through. Along with all of the techniques this can be used for other types of finish too and I look at it in more detail later in the chapter when considering desert finishes. The other masking methods are similar with the main difference being the masking medium. Crushed salt crystals applied to a slightly damp model surface are another way to achieve the masking and there are even methods involving toothpaste and Marmite (for those who haven't come across this, it's a strongly tasting, thick and dark spread for sandwiches and toast!). I've only seen the Marmite method used once in a magazine article so it doesn't appear to be too popular.

This early Tiger I had a patchily sprayed application of white over the base grey. The worn areas were reproduced by a combination of dry brushing and hand-painted chips and scratches.

This Panzer IV was a model I built for my first Osprey book. Both the base colour and the thinly applied white are enamels with an acrylic varnish layer in between. This layer prevents the thinners from attacking the base colour.

HAIRSPRAY TECHNIQUE

More recently a method involving hairspray has become increasingly popular for achieving worn finishes. I first saw this on a Bergepanther spade at one of the UK's big shows, Euromilitaire, around 2004. It belonged to Phil Stutcinskas and he'd used a technique involving several layers of hairspray under different layers of colour. The hairspray when dampened allows the colour above to be scraped and rubbed away. Since then many modellers have successfully used this method to create some stunning worn effects. I've tried the method myself over single-colour and multiple-colour camouflages and it works just as well for both. The most dramatic effects are when there is a greater contrast so dark colours like the grey on early war German armour is very effective when combined with a whitewash. I've also used it to good effect on late-war, hard-edged three colour schemes. If applying it over a single lighter colour I tend to make that colour a little darker than normal to give it a bit more contrast with the white.

So let's take a look at the steps involved in the hairspray technique. My advice is to try it out on an old model first. This will give you a feel for how much hairspray to apply as too little will make it very difficult to remove the white later on. Too much and the white can come away too easily. It will also let you experiment with how different methods can be used to remove the white in different ways – to create chips, scratches or softer rubbed-off areas. To start, the model needs to be at the point where the main colours have all been applied and

The first step of the hairspray technique involves painting the model in its base camouflage colours. This Panzer IV Ausf. F has been painted in Humbrol dark grey enamel. The markings have been applied, in this case Archer dry transfers, and the model sealed with a single application of Johnson's Klear acrylic varnish.

A couple of moderately heavy layers of hairspray have been applied over the whole model.

A thin, patchy coat of acrylic white paint has been sprayed over the base grey colour.

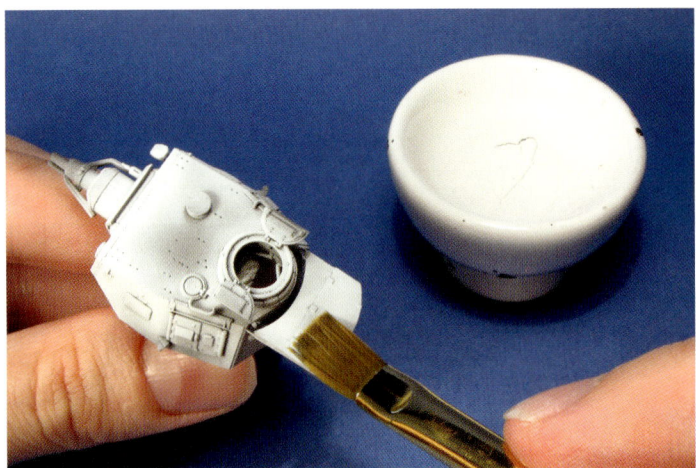

In order to start wearing away the white paint, apply water to small sections of the model at a time.

After a couple of minutes, the water will soften the hairspray underneath the paint. Using a small cut-down brush, small areas of white can be carefully removed.

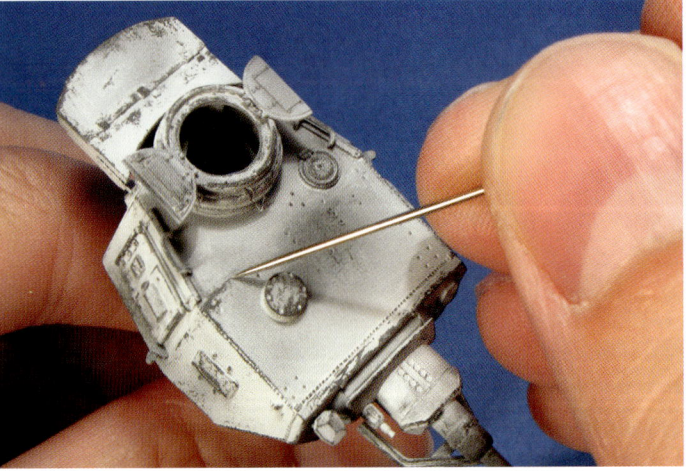

To achieve fine scratches and chips apply some more water and drag the tip of a needle lightly across the surface. This needs to be done carefully to avoid scratching the base colour.

Softer contrasts between the grey and white can be achieved by lightly dry brushing grey with a flat brush. This gives a subtle worn-down effect.

The technique is equally good for any base colour. This late version Hetzer has a three-colour hard-edged camouflage pattern underneath. I kept the application of white very thin, leaving the colours underneath partly visible in areas. It's ready now for weathering and shading.

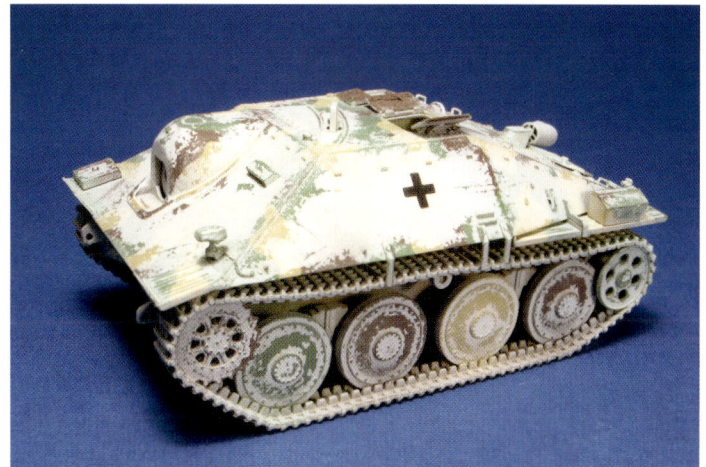

A dilute wash of Humbrol Dark Earth (29) and a small amount of burnt umber oil paint is applied over the whole model. This wash tones down the harshness of the white and breaks it up a little.

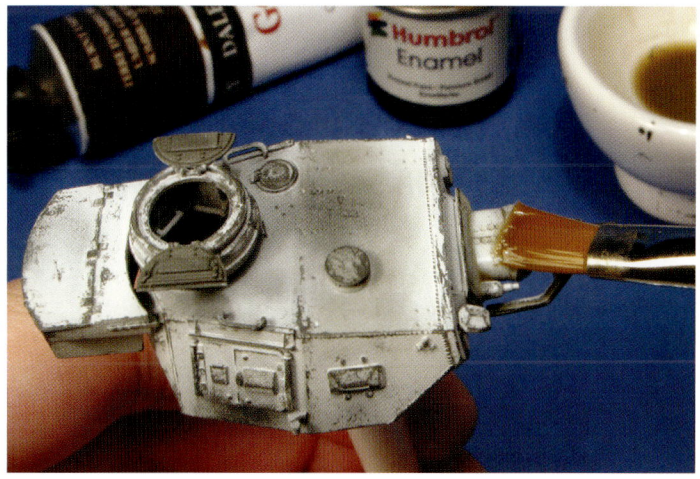

had time to fully set. If there are any markings that need to be applied then this is the time to add them. Whitewash can often be seen painted around the markings to leave them visible and we can add that effect as part of the later steps. In some cases temporary markings are applied on top of the white and again these can easily be represented later. The act of removing the white isn't particularly rough but to ensure the paint and markings remain intact underneath I usually apply some Klear first. The hairspray can now be applied and I've used a few different brands all equally successfully.

This part can be quite daunting, especially the first time as it seems strange to be spraying it over a model. Even after trying this a number of times I still paint some spare parts in parallel to the main model to allow me to test each step out on those first. It's not a good idea to spray directly from the can as it doesn't allow for fine control and can lead to the model being swamped in hairspray. I spray some into a small cup first and then pour this into my airbrush. One of the lessons I learned early on is that what might look like a thick coat will mostly evaporate away, so although you shouldn't be overly zealous with the application, don't be too hesitant. My very first attempt was too cautious and I had a lot of trouble getting the paint to wear off later. At least this was on a

practice model. I've found that a couple of moderately heavy coats with a few minutes' break between them results in the optimum covering – hairspray is quite volatile and it doesn't take long for it to dry. Layering the white coat is the next step and this doesn't have to be done straight away. You can leave it overnight if you wish but I usually get straight to work. I've used Revell and Vallejo acrylic white so far and both work well. Keeping the white well thinned makes it easy to spray a patchy finish and to gradually build this up. It doesn't matter if you make multiple passes over an area with the white as it will still wear away without any problems.

One of the things I like about this technique is that each step doesn't require waiting for more than a few minutes until you can start the next. Some painting methods require much longer waits in between, hours or even days which can be frustrating when you're keen to make progress. Conversely I found that if you do have to put things away to work on the next day then this isn't a problem either.

To start, I pour some warm tap water into a small bowl and line up a few brushes. A large flat brush is ideal for painting the water onto the model's surface. A medium-sized brush and a finer brush that are both cut down to a stumpy shape are used to remove the white paint. A pin or needle and a sharpened toothpick are also useful

to have at hand for making small scrapes and scratches. Apply the water to small sections of the model at a time and allow it to soak and start dissolving the hairspray. As the hairspray softens the white retains less of a hold on the model and if after leaving it for a minute or two the white still refuses to move then flood a bit more water over the area. Once it has softened, gentle scrubbing with one of the cut-down brushes will cause the white paint to start to rub off. If you used a lot of hairspray then it will tend to pull off larger chips of paint. When you're happy with the effect in the area you're currently working in dab any remaining water away and the paint will regain its grip again.

As I mentioned earlier you can leave this overnight and by reapplying water it's possible to continue with the paint removal at a later time. When the larger areas have been treated I then turn to using a needle or cocktail stick to recreate the finer scratches. Again applying water to the surface and gently dragging the needle/cocktail stick along it will pull very thin areas of paint away.

This is particularly useful for vehicles with *Schürzen* that can brush against branches or other sharp items resulting in long scrapes and scratches. At this point the hairspray step can be considered complete but I usually turn to additional methods to complement

Shadows around the smaller details can be strengthened by applying a dark pin-wash. Wetting the area around the details with Humbrol thinners first will help with this.

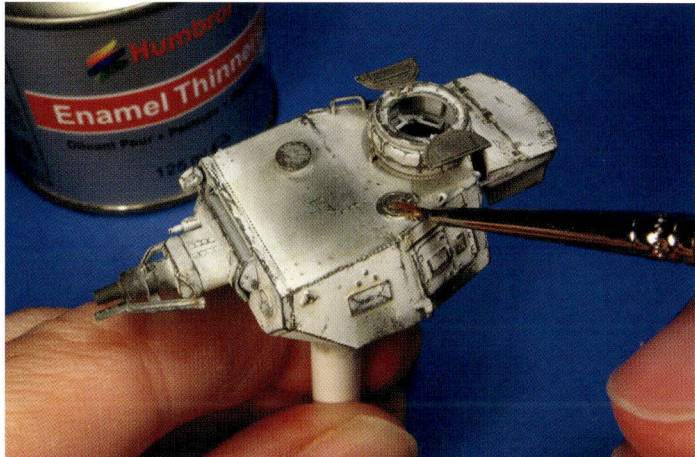

Next, a dilute black wash is dotted around the detail – the previous application of thinners help draw the wash around it.

Acrylic white is used to add fine highlights along the edges of some of the scratches and paint chips.

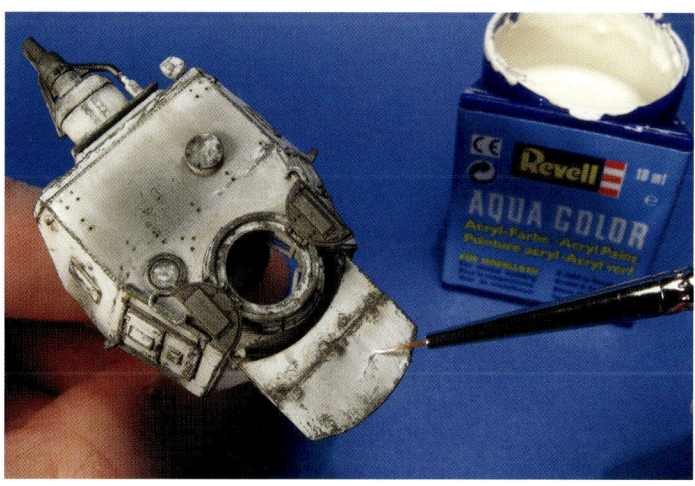

A dirty brown wash of Humbrol Light Earth (119) is applied on the horizontal surfaces to add depth to the grimy finish.

At this point the smaller details such as tools and other equipment are painted.

A black pencil is useful for darkening the edges where the white paint has worn away.

The final step is to represent streaks and areas of rust. Use a small brush to add small dots of burnt umber oil paint to a few areas of the model.

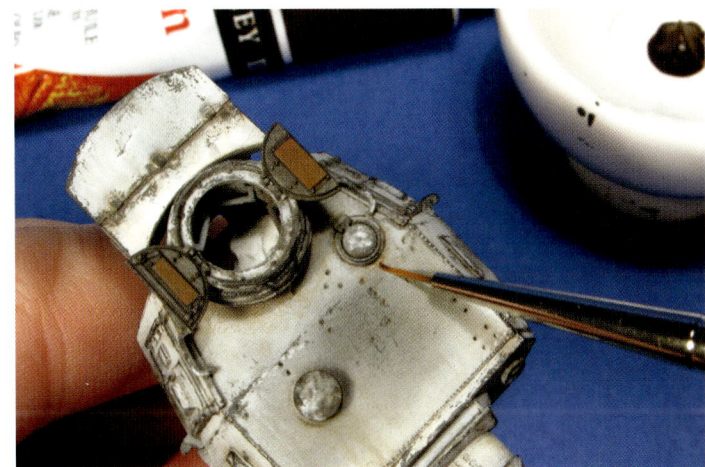

Using a clean brush dipped in thinners, drag down the oil paint to represent subtle rust streaks. It's important not to overdo this step. Now the whitewash is done and figures, stowage and any remaining items can be added.

it. Dry brushing has fallen out of favour in recent times but I still find it a useful technique for creating softer areas of whitewash that has worn away. As the hairspray approach gives hard-edged boundaries, dry brushing will give a softer contrast to this. Larger horizontal surfaces that might suffer from light wear can be represented well by dry brushing.

Once this is complete I turn to my usual methods of shading and weathering the model. An overall dilute wash works well in toning down the brightness of the white and breaking it up into a more patchy effect. Dark pin-washes will add strong shadow and pull some of the detail back to prominence. Other effects such as rust and oil streaks also work particularly well against the white as do muddy finishes around the lower hull and running gear. A final note about this approach is that there is no need to seal the model with varnish either before the wash is applied or at the end of the weathering unless you wish to do this anyway.

RECREATING A WORN DESERT FINISH

Achieving a worn look to vehicles that serve in a desert environment can be done in much the same way as that for whitewashed vehicles. In some cases vehicles will have lighter colours applied over the darker colours that they are usually to be found in. These will suffer badly over time in the extreme heat and abrasive conditions. Darker-coloured vehicles may also be hastily painted over with mud and this will dry to a pale colour. It will then quickly start to wear and rub off. Even without additional applications of paint or mud, heavy layers of dust will build up and cause dark vehicles to gradually blend into the environment more and more.

The dust will quickly rub off certain areas, revealing the colours underneath again. I'm going to look at a method to reproduce this that I briefly mentioned when discussing whitewashes – the use of masking methods, or more precisely Maskol liquid latex. The example I use will illustrate a thin layer of dust and sand covering the entire vehicle that has worn away in patches. This is illustrated with a modern Israeli vehicle, the Achzarit, painted using Humbrol enamels.

The model received a couple of airbrushed coats of Humbrol enamel and once done I started applying the Maskol. There are other brands of similar masking agents available and these are probably just as good but this

There are many brands of liquid latex masking agent and Humbrol produce one for modellers called Maskol. After painting the base colour, I applied Maskol with a small strip of kitchen scouring material with the fibres teased out.

A dust colour has been airbrushed over the entire vehicle, keeping the application light and patchy. Once this was dry, I removed the Maskol to reveal the darker base colour underneath.

Dry brushing a mix of the dust colour and base colour over the model will blend the two colours together. The Maskol treatment will leave a hard-edged boundary and this will soften it a little.

Using the base colour and a fine brush, I painted along edges and around the hatches to supplement the Maskol effect. The dust would quickly wear away from these areas.

particular one is made by Humbrol and is easy to find in the UK. A good way of applying the Maskol is to use a small piece of material from a household scouring pad. These are made of a rough, fibrous material for tough cleaning jobs and it's best to tease the fibres out a little before using them. I hold the strip in tweezers and dip it into the Maskol. You'll need to move quite quickly once this is done as it only remains workable for a short time.

It's also best to only apply a small amount at a time as too much on the pad will result in blobs of Maskol on the model rather than a more realistic and delicate pattern. If you do put too much on it can be removed from the model easily enough and reapplied. By teasing the pad out to different degrees you can vary the effect and it's worth experimenting a bit with this first. Focus more on areas most likely to be worn away such as those with

moving parts or where the crew would be most active. When you're happy with this and the Maskol has dried it's time to layer on the next coat of paint. At this point the model will look very messy but keep with it. I mix a pale dust colour and concentrate it more on the horizontal surfaces where dust will settle more. When the paint is completely dry you can remove the Maskol. There are a number of ways to do this and I use tweezers

The completed model after a series of washes and other weathering steps. This view clearly shows the mottled pattern of dust that covers the model, being more concentrated around raised detail.

to gently pull away the large areas. If you find some is left behind then a bit of dried Maskol or Blu-Tack on the end of a cocktail stick can be useful in pulling it away. When it has all been removed you should be left with a nicely mottled effect of the lighter colour over the darker base. Unlike some of the other methods for achieving these kinds of finishes the extent of the effect is fixed early on when the Maskol is applied. You can tweak the finish, however, and paint in more of the

base colour with a fine brush if you need to. You may also find that the contrast between the colours looks too harsh at this point but the next steps will help blend these and give a more natural look. Overall dry brushing in the base colour will help to blend the finish also and tone down the dustiness of the finish.

OTHER EFFECTS

There are other specialized finishes that the methods described above can be applied to. One of the bigger challenges in modelling military vehicles is the representation of a heavily damaged or destroyed vehicle.

Realistically portraying burnt-out areas isn't particularly easy but it's also not out of reach for any modeller. Constructing the model will also be more challenging too and in most cases you may need to add some interior details, especially if the vehicle has it engine deck, turret or other large sections blown away. Regarding the finish itself, I've built a couple of knocked-out vehicles both with large burnt and rusted areas. Both of these used different finishing techniques and pre-dated my use of Maskol and the hairspray methods. One day I plan to make version three of a destroyed vehicle using the hairspray method.

This was my first attempt at a burnt-out vehicle. It's Revell's Panzer IV Ausf. H kit with some resin interior parts from Extratech. It features a scratch-built fighting compartment and turret interior. I painted it using the pre-shading technique by applying an overall coat of black followed by patchy overspray of rusty colours. A number of rusty washes finished the effect.

My second attempt at a destroyed vehicle was a bit more ambitious with all of the interior parts scratch-built. To achieve the appearance of burnt areas along with areas of original colour I painted the base colours first and then airbrushed the rusty areas on top. As soon as this was dry I blended the edges with a small brush dipped in thinners.

This whitewashed Hetzer was painted using the hairspray technique not only for the main finish but also for the rusty exhaust. In fact the technique can be used for any multi-layered effect where you want a harder edge between the different colours.

PRESENTATION

Once I've made the finishing touches to my latest model I'll probably take a number of final photos of it and then mount it on a small base. Even just a plain wooden base with no groundwork and a simple nameplate can really make a difference to the presentation of the model. A good analogy with this is a well-finished painting – it will usually look better with a frame around it rather than just being left plain. Adding a little groundwork can add another dimension to the model and give it some additional context. In both of these cases a base will also protect the model from handling that can lead to fingerprints or broken parts. I'm going to look at the simpler situations of setting the model off with firstly a plain base and then one with a modicum of groundwork. The creation of small vignettes or grand dioramas is something out of the scope of this book and they are almost separate art forms in themselves. Finally I'll describe how I take my photographs – including the ones in this book – and show how even on a budget you can achieve some great results.

PLAIN BASES

For most of my models I finish them by mounting them on a plain wooden base with a nameplate. I greatly admire those modellers who can create vast, intricate dioramas with many elements that all fit so well together. Some of the best scenes I've seen have been small vignettes with a little groundwork and a few figures. Some of these can really draw you in by being historically accurate and telling an interesting story. My own real enjoyment though is the construction and painting of the vehicles and I've never really been interested in spending time on groundwork and other periphery – I could be starting my next model instead! Still, it's something that I think I may focus on more someday. I've also seen well-made models on poor bases and these detract from the work

rather than enhance it. For now I'm happy displaying my work on compact, plain bases with a descriptive nameplate to set it off and give some context.

My first bases were homemade attempts using squared-off pieces of plain wood. I experimented with painting them a single colour, varnishing and also waxing them. In all these cases it took time and effort to create the base and I was never truly happy with the results. As I became more serious about modelling I found it was taking longer and longer to finish each one, until I was only building a handful per year. This is still the case and after devoting so much time to each I feel the more expensive option of buying a ready made base is more than worth it. There are many companies that sell finished bases in a bewildering range of shapes, styles and finishes.

If these are not enough then many also offer custom services that cost a bit more but will give you a base that will precisely fit any need. There is also a choice in material with many different types of wood available or even other materials such as MDF, an artificially created substance made largely from wood. Almost more than anything else the choice you make in your selection is highly personal. My own preference is for rectangular mahogany bases that just fit the dimensions of the model. In terms of finish I like a plain satin black. Varnished wood, especially darker varieties, can look very attractive but in a way I think they can distract the eye from the model itself. Choosing black gives good contrast to the model and its plain appearance will lead the viewer's eye to focus more on the model. I think a glossy finish can also be a

As well as making your own wooden bases there are plenty of options for buying them readymade. Many companies offer a standard range of shapes and sizes along with a customization service for very specific requirements.

A couple of well-placed metal pins or short lengths of thick wire can secure a model to its base. I pick an area under each track run that is directly below a wheel and drill a hole. For wheeled vehicles just pick any wheel on each side.

A length of wire has been inserted here that just sticks proud of the track surface. This needs to be repeated on the other side.

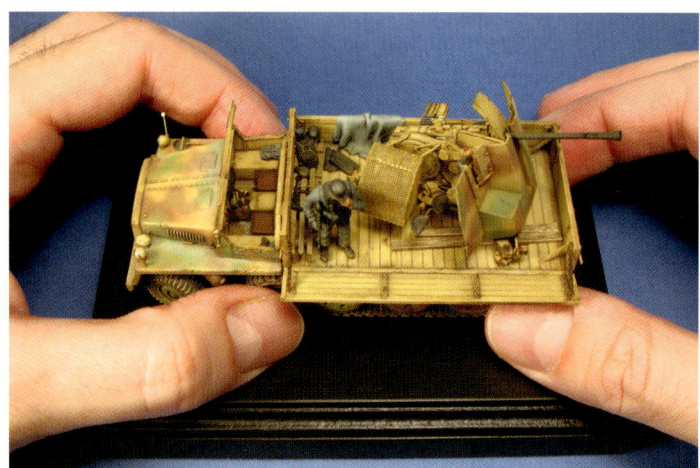

Positioning the model on the base and gently applying some downwards pressure will leave two small marks from the lengths of wire in the track.

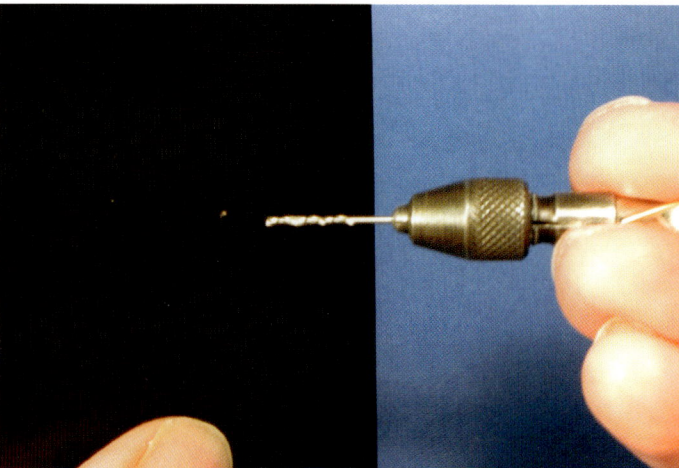

Drill into the base at the location of the two marks.

Two longer sections of wire are glued into the holes in the base. The model can now be attached to these to secure it firmly but temporarily.

bit distracting with its shine and reflections, whereas a matt one seems to attract or show more marks. Matt bases just don't seem to have the smoothness and pleasing effect of a satin finish. I order mine (both standard and custom-made sizes) from Wiremill Designs in the UK. Full contact details are given in the final chapter and, although they deliver to other countries, similar companies can no doubt be found throughout the world.

Once you've selected a suitable base you need to decide how to attach the model to it. I would never recommend just plonking the model on top without any means of attachment as this is just asking for the model to slide off and fall to the floor. I was at a major model show some years back and saw the remains of a beautifully made model that had slipped off its base whilst being judged in the competition. Gluing the model to the base would avoid problems like this but feels a bit too severe. If you do plan to visit shows with your models this can make it more difficult and you might also want to change the base in the future. My preferred choice is to attach the model with a couple of wire pins. These will hold the model steadily enough to withstand the base being picked up and viewed but will also allow the model to be removed for storage or travelling.

Nameplates are another item that you can make either for yourself or buy from a dedicated company. I used to make mine from strips of black plastic with white dry transfer lettering. Painting this with satin varnish gave a protective, smooth finish. This was in the days before high-quality colour PC printers and nowadays it's possible to print out professional-looking plates yourself. As with bases I've ended up settling on buying them from a specialist nameplate company, this being Name It! They are well known in the UK and attend many model shows with examples of the plates they offer. They also provide overseas delivery and details are given in the last chapter. The plates I buy are very well priced and as the quality and service is very good I've never looked elsewhere. They have a strong two-sided adhesive pre-applied to the rear to make attaching them to the model easy.

ADDING SOME GROUNDWORK

I mentioned my preference earlier for using plain bases but there have been occasions where I've added some groundwork. Some kinds of subject, a destroyed vehicle being a good example, need some groundwork more so than other models. If you look at pictures of burnt-out vehicles you'll see lots of damaged parts and debris strewn on the ground around the vehicle

Adding a nameplate to a base is important in giving some identity to the finished model. As with the bases you can make your own or turn to specialist companies to do it for you. These examples are from a UK company called Name It! They offer a variety of finishes, colours and fonts. A gloss black plate with silver lettering is my preferred choice.

I had this plain black base custom made to fit the model. As I was going to use household filler to model some groundwork, I roughened up the surface to give something for the filler to grip on to.

The edges of the base have been masked off and some pre-mixed filler is being layered onto it. Make sure you use crack-resistant, non-shrinking filler. If there is any shrinkage it will slowly warp the base over time.

The back of a knife is useful in smoothing the filler over the base and giving it a more even covering.

The weight of a real vehicle will create marks in the ground. To represent this, the model can be gently pushed into the filler before it has fully set. To prevent any filler from getting on the model, cover the groundwork with some cling film first.

Tyre marks can be made by rolling a tyre over the filler.

Once the filler is dry, some texture is added to it by gluing fine sand and pieces of cat litter in random places. White PVA glue is suitable for this.

The finished base before painting.

I began painting the base by giving it a pre-shading coat of black enamel.

A sand colour has been airbrushed over the base leaving some of the darker colour showing through.

A dark brown enamel wash will help accentuate the details.

Small rocks and pebbles can be picked out in a light grey colour.

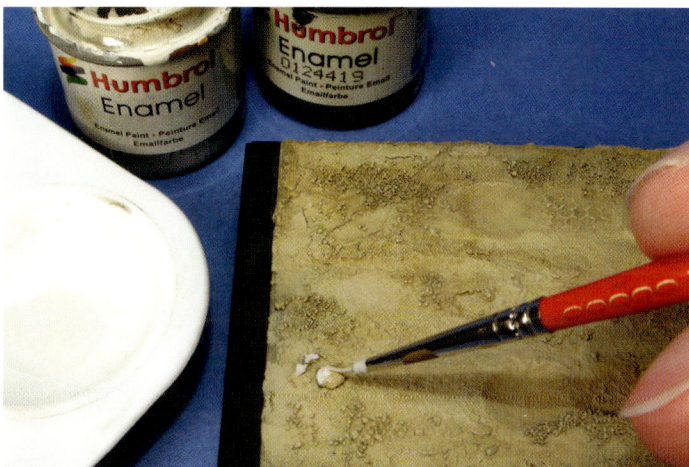

A black pin-wash is applied around the details to give them some additional depth and shadow.

The finished base with the model pinned to it.

and so some groundwork will be necessary when modelling this type of scene. Even simple groundwork can take many forms: mud, sand, tarmac, snow and ice, water, etc. and there are far too many to cover here. I'm going to just select one, probably one of the simplest and something that anyone new to creating groundwork could start with very easily. A dusty desert scene can be created with a minimum of materials in a short time but introduces a few ideas that can be applied to any type of groundwork.

PHOTOGRAPHY

Taking photographs of your in-progress and finished models is a great way to capture the work you put into them for posterity. Posting pictures of your work on the many modelling websites are a great way to get feedback on the things you are doing right and the things you are doing wrong. Creating a personal modelling-related website can be a satisfying endeavour too, giving you an opportunity to showcase your work to the world. If you want to write modelling articles then the subject of photography is really unavoidable. Two other benefits I've found from taking frequent photos of my modelling work are that the pictures can often show up issues that I would have normally missed, giving you a chance to fix them. It also allows you to keep a detailed visual record of the work that went into the construction of a model. Without photos and once covered in paint it's easy to forget the precise nature of the work you put into a model. Sometimes I return to a specific subject years after building a different variant and it can be useful being able to see the work I put into the first model.

Model photography involves getting close to your subject and this is particularly true for small-scale models. In fact sometimes you may want to get as close as 1cm from a model and this poses its own problems in terms of lighting, focus and other issues. I'm far from being a professional photographer and apart from the camera I use, my setup and other equipment such as lighting and backdrops are all bargain basement items. If there are any professional photographers reading this then much of the following will appear very basic – so you may want to skip this chapter! Still, I've reached a standard that has allowed me to write numerous magazine articles and a few books.

CAMERA

Without hesitation I'd say the biggest development that opened photography up for taking model photos was the advent of affordable digital cameras. As with other areas of modelling, practice is essential and the ability to quickly try out new things and get instant feedback is very important. The time-consuming process of using film which involved getting it processed, realizing you weren't happy with the results and then having to repeat it all again with tweaked camera settings or lighting are now long gone thankfully. With a digital camera you can take a photo, immediately see if it's worth keeping and fiddle around with the settings to try and improve the next one. What may have taken weeks of experimentation, and of course additional expense with film, can be condensed down into hours.

My photography setup is very basic to say the least. I don't have enough space to set up a permanent area so I go for the simplest approach with the least amount of equipment I can get away with.

Another big benefit of digital cameras is their ability to take close-up photographs. Most of them, even those at the cheaper end of the point-and-shoot market, have macro modes that allow you to get very close to your subject, in many cases just a few centimetres away. This is ideal for model photography where to fill the frame with the subject will require these sorts of distances. With film cameras the only real option years ago was to buy an expensive SLR camera and a macro lens to go with it. Many years back I found an affordable fixed-lens film camera from a company called Goko. This was the Goko MacroMax and was specially designed for very close-up macro work. It could get some good results but wasn't very consistent in this respect. It usually took many rolls of film to get a handful of very good photos.

So which digital camera is best? There is of course no single answer to this question and even if there was it would frequently be changing due to the rapid pace of technology. Probably the biggest decision you need to make is whether you want an SLR camera or a simpler point-and-shoot. SLR cameras are the choice of professionals and serious amateurs. Your budget will be the biggest factor in the choice you make here as they are quite an investment financially.

The major difference between the two types is that SLRs allow for much more physical customization with the ability to fit a variety of different specialized lenses. Before the advent of digital cameras, another big benefit was that SLRs gave a true though the lens picture whilst point-and-shoots suffered from parallax problems at close up. This meant you actually saw a slightly different image through a non-SLR camera than you would ultimately get in the final photo. With large digital LCD preview screens on almost all digital cameras nowadays this tends not to be such a differentiating factor any more. I've found that high-end point-and-shoot cameras share many of the capabilities of SLRs and for me I find them perfectly adequate for the job.

I've had experience with two of the major brands, Nikon and Canon, and would recommend them both. There are a number of key factors you should consider first when buying a camera. The first and most obvious perhaps is the resolution of the images it will take and these are given as mega pixel (million pixels) values. The greater the value the larger the images will be when viewed on a monitor. For posting images on the Internet the resolution does not have to be particularly high with 1 MP almost filling a 17-in. monitor set at a 1280 by 800 resolution. In terms of printing, the higher the

resolution the larger the image can be printed whilst still maintaining its sharpness. For magazines and books a higher resolution than you would use on the Internet is needed, at the very least 3 MP. For larger-print images such as a book or magazine cover you would really be looking for 5 MP at least. These days even the cheapest cameras have values greater than these so the pixel resolution is unlikely to be an issue. Probably the most important thing to look for is a macro setting that will allow you to get in-focus close ups. This is again something that the majority of digital cameras now provide. The quality of the lens is another very important factor. Usually you can rely on the big names such as Canon and Nikon to provide high-quality lenses in their various models. My best piece of advice would be to thoroughly check out as many online or in-print reviews as you can. As a good camera is a major investment it's wise to find out as much as you can about those you are considering. There are many photography websites and forums that are worth checking out too and they will have a wealth of information on the subject.

All the digital cameras I have owned and used for taking model photos have been high-end point-and-shoots and I'm still to use an SLR camera. I'll probably only take that step when I feel dissatisfied with the results I'm getting. The term Prosumer is sometimes used for these kinds of top range non-SLRs. They sit somewhere between a standard all-purpose family camera and a fully featured SLR. They have great flexibility in the manual settings they provide, often comparable to SLR cameras in many respects. The most noticeable difference with SLRs is the lack of a changeable lens. My first digital camera was a 3 MP Nikon 885 and I used this for my first Osprey book. Following on from this I purchased a 5 MP Nikon 5400. Although the resolution increase was a big benefit, the colour reproduction and general image quality were also improved. These types of improvements are often overshadowed in marketing literature, which tends to focus on pixel counts and zoom ranges. My third and current camera is a 12 MP Canon Powershot G9.

I've been very impressed with this camera as it provides a great degree of flexibility when set to manual control. It also features superb colour reproduction and the internal image-processing software is the same as that on Canon's SLR cameras of the same period. Having the extra pixels to play with is also a big benefit of course and I'll return to this point later. The current model is the G12 and no doubt this will have been superseded by the time this book is published. I've no doubt that the 'G' range will continue to provide excellent cameras for model photography for some time.

Tripod

Although a good camera is essential for taking high-quality photos it's equally important that you have a good photography setup. A tripod to hold your camera still is a necessity as any shake or wobble will blur the image, making it useless. Tripods can be picked up cheaply and there's no need to buy anything expensive. In fact anything that holds the camera completely still will do. When I first started taking pictures of my models I even resorted to resting the camera on a pile of books – at least until I had a chance to go out and purchase a tripod! Do make sure the tripod is adjustable enough for your needs, as you may want to set the height and angles to get a variety of different shot types. Mine usually range from dramatic eye-level shots to those directly from above that show the overall model. I also own a mini-tripod that sits on the desk with the model. This has a limited range in height but is more convenient to store and handle due to its small size.

Backgrounds

The choice of background has a big effect on the appearance of photos and I aim to use those that

I have a homemade backdrop created from two pieces of wood glued at right angles to each other. Between them is taped a curved sheet of thin card. This semi-portable contraption can be stored elsewhere and just placed on a desk when I need to take some photos. Other background colours can also be draped over the top quite easily.

will cause the least distraction from the model itself. Curving a piece of paper or card so that it runs gradually from lying horizontally to vertically will create an infinity curve, resulting in a featureless backdrop. Smooth grained card or thick paper is good for this and unless you have some space dedicated to photography then you'll need to set this up each time you want to take some photos.

This is a problem I have, so to avoid repeated setting up I've made a small portable backdrop that is stored away most of the time. It can then be brought out when needed. For this I just glued two rectangular pieces of wood at right angles to each other to create a sturdy frame and taped a curved sheet of thin blue card between them. The wood pieces are actually just cheap kitchen chopping boards although any similarly sized off-cuts of wood will do the trick. Different-coloured card can also be placed over the piece initially attached to the wooden frame. In terms of colour I lean towards a mid-blue for in-progress photos as it's a pleasant neutral colour that most other colours look good against. For finished models I've used various colours but recently I've started just using plain white. One benefit of a very light colour such as this is that it reflects more of the light. The quality of lighting is of paramount importance, as I will mention again later.

LIGHTING

Lighting is as important as the quality of the camera. I probably have the cheapest setup possible using just plain desktop lamps and bulbs. The light from these will cast strong shadows so in order to soften that I tape a piece of tracing paper over each lamp to diffuse the light. The colour from standard bulbs will cause close-up photos to have a yellowish tinge to them and before the advent of digital cameras and digital home processing I used daylight-balanced bulbs. Most digital cameras will allow you to correct for these undesirable colour casts by providing 'white balance' settings.

A built-in auto-balance can be used to automatically adjust the images but some also have a number of pre-defined settings for different lighting conditions. These might include fluorescent, daylight, overcast and incandescent light. Higher end cameras may also have a completely manual white balance option where you can use a pure white item, for example a piece of card to calibrate the camera's setting.

The positioning of the lights is also important and I have a top 60-watt light shining directly down but slightly in front of the model and a 40-watt light set almost level with it, offset to the front to provide a fill-in light. This gives good lighting of the side and top of the model, ensuring there are no areas in complete darkness. One thing I'd

warn against is the use of camera flash. Using this can give an unnatural and flat look to your pictures, losing the finesse of the finish and weathering. I'm also not a fan of outdoor photography using natural sunlight. The main problem is the lack of control of the lighting. Plus here in the UK we get many overcast and wet days – so that rules out any outdoor photography!

DIGITAL IMAGE FORMATS

There are many digital image formats around each with their own pros and cons. For digital cameras three of these are common, with JPEG being by far the most popular. The JPEG format (with files ending with a .jpg extension) is particularly good from a storage point of view as it can be compressed to very small files sizes, thereby allowing many images to be stored on a memory card. The down side of this is that image quality can suffer if compressed too much. Compression is applied to the image data in order to make the file size small and the type used here is known as 'lossy' compression as some of the image data will be lost. The amount of compression can be controlled, however, and there will usually be several settings allowing you to adjust this. Any deterioration in image quality at low compression will only be visible at high magnification. Another format that some higher-end cameras support is the TIFF format. These files, ending in a .tif or .tiff extension, can either have no compression at all or some low-level 'lossless' compression that won't affect the image quality. In either case the file sizes will suffer and an image saved as a TIFF will be much larger than a JPEG equivalent. However, memory card space has become cheap as time has gone on and so space issues aren't as much of a problem any more. Plus when taking model photos at home, it's easy enough to transfer the photos from a full memory card to your computer and clear it down again.

The final type of format commonly found in cameras is the RAW format and this is usually found in more expensive cameras such as DSLRs and high-end point and shoot models. Digital cameras run their own internal image-processing software and will use this to sharpen, adjust contrast levels, modify white balance and tweak other settings on the images they take. As such they will have a good set of default values for these when working in auto-mode. In manual mode these settings can be adjusted by the user but will still be irreversibly applied to the images if in JPEG or TIFF format. The RAW format takes up a lot of space but represents the image as the camera actually sees it – before it's had a chance to process it in software. RAW files need to be

opened up in special software (supplied with the camera) but once there they can be viewed in their most basic form. The software will allow you to modify the settings you used to initially take the photo, in essence allowing you to return to the point where the image was taken.

GETTING THE RIGHT CAMERA SETTINGS

Once you've got hold of a suitable camera, tripod, backdrop and lights you can start experimenting with the camera settings. On those with a full manual mode you'll often find additional ones such as Aperture Priority and Shutter Priority. My preference is Aperture Priority. The aperture is simply the hole that lets light into the camera. Aperture Priority allows you to set the size of this, which for close-up macro shots will have a large effect on the amount of the image that remains in focus. The smaller the aperture, the more of the model will remain sharply in focus. The technical term for this is the 'depth of field'. The trade off is that a smaller aperture lets in less light so a longer exposure time is needed. This isn't a problem for this type of photography as the model remains still and the camera is fixed on a tripod. In contrast to this some types of photography such as outdoor action shots at sports events for example involve a fast-moving subject and perhaps

a camera just held by hand and subject to camera shake. This type of photo is best taken with shutter priority where a fast shutter speed will prevent motion blur of the moving object. This will open up the aperture and let a lot more light in within a given time. It will also reduce the depth of field but this is less of a problem the further away the subject is. One thing to note is that the aperture size is set based on an f-stop value. The higher this value, the smaller the aperture.

A full array of manual or semi-manual settings can appear quite intimidating if you're used to auto shooting modes but there are a handful that if set correctly will help you get some good results. Turning the macro mode on is an absolute must. The auto focus on most good cameras will also be enough and I've never resorted to manual focusing. Getting the white balance correct is also very important, especially for macro photography. The auto white balance wasn't always good enough on my older cameras and I would use manual calibration of this using a piece of white card. This involves pointing the camera at the card and pushing a button to let it know that the object filling its view should appear as pure white. On the Canon camera I've found the Tungsten (Incandescent) setting to give good results, although on rare occasions I tweak the appearance a bit in software afterwards. Metering is the process that the camera uses to determine how exposed the final image should be. With Aperture Priority mode set, this essentially sets the exposure time. Several of the more common options here are Matrix Metering, Spot Metering and Centre-Weighted Metering. There are also others, some of which are variants on these but these three are the common ones. Each uses a different method to determine the correct level of exposure needed to give a well-exposed (i.e. not too dark or too light) image. Often Matrix Metering is the default setting and this samples various points throughout the whole image to determine its overall level of brightness. Based on this it then chooses the best exposure time. This is useful in most general situations where there are no large, overly dark or bright areas within the image. Taking a model photo against a white background using this setting can result in the model appearing dark and under exposed. This is because the camera would reduce its exposure time to counteract the large bright white areas. Conversely a black background would be detected as giving too dark an image and the camera would compensate by increasing the exposure time. This would lighten the appearance of the black background and over expose the model. Because of this I find Spot and Centre-Weighted

metering options the most suitable for model photography. Both of these give a higher weight to a specific region of the frame. In Spot Metering this is within a very small area and although often at the centre some cameras allow this region to be moved around. Centre-Weighted Metering gives a higher weight (typically 60 to 80 per cent) to a region at the centre of the frame and the remainder to the surrounding areas. This is my preferred option in most cases.

There are still the odd occasions when the image appears under or over exposed to some degree and this is where Exposure Compensation can be used. This allows both positive and negative increments to account for both cases and allows you to get just the right exposure. Traditional camera film has a fixed ISO rating and this determines its sensitivity, or 'speed'. Higher values such as 400 or 800 are suited to low light conditions or action shots where the amount of light hitting the film will be low. The down side is that the images will appear grainier the higher the ISO setting of the film. Lower speed film such as 64 and 100 will give a less grainy image with better colour resolution but require longer exposure times. Although digital cameras work in a different way they still have an ISO equivalent value that can be set. In a digital camera a higher ISO setting results in more image

noise that is comparable with the graininess of traditional film. Always choose the lowest your camera provides and on mine this is 80. A final point to bear in mind is that even with a tripod the act of carefully pushing the button on the camera to take a picture can cause a tiny amount of shake. To avoid this some cameras allow for a remote shutter release to be attached so you can push a button on this instead and take a picture without touching the camera directly. I just use the camera's self-timer though which is something almost all cameras provide. One or two seconds is plenty for straightforward shots of just the model itself. For photos involving my hands (such as those illustrating step-by-step examples) I use a longer self-timer value as this gives time to get myself in the right position for the shot.

For completeness I've listed the settings I use on my camera. On a good-quality camera most or all of these should be available.

- Macro mode
- Auto focus
- Incandescent White Balance Setting
- Aperture Priority
- F-stop 8.0 (highest)
- Centre-Weighted Metering
- ISO 80 (lowest)
- RAW image format
- Camera self-timer (two to ten seconds)

OTHER TRICKS

There are a couple of other tricks to be aware of that can improve the quality of your photos. Depth of field and resulting blur problems become increasingly strong the closer you get to the model. Moving it further back will allow more of it to remain in focus. Pixel counts have rapidly increased since the introduction of digital cameras and this has given the photographer more pixels to play with. Because of this you can move a model further back from the lens to achieve a better depth of field and just crop the image later. The amount you can do this naturally depends on the amount of pixels your camera supports and on how big you'd like your final image to be. The optimum image size depends on what you intend to do with it. As mentioned earlier, more pixels are needed if you wish to print high-quality hard copies of your photos, whereas for the Internet you can get away with using lower values.

Another simple trick is based on the 'two-thirds rule'. This states that when a camera is focussing at a specific distance, one-third of the area in focus will be in front of that and two-thirds will be behind it. Based on this you should aim to focus on a point about one-third back from the part of the model closest to the camera. This will give the greatest chance of getting an all-in-focus model.

This image suffers from two main problems; a poor white balance giving it a yellowish cast and a camera that wasn't set to macro mode. The second issue makes the model appear blurred.

With the white balance corrected and the macro mode turned on the image is better but a low f-stop value (large aperture) and a focal point at the rear of the model means most of the picture is still blurry.

ARTICLE WRITING

To wrap up this chapter I'll briefly mention writing modelling articles. This is something that I encourage all modellers to consider. You may not have any interest in this but if you do and the only thing stopping you is confidence then read on.

My own experience started by writing a few articles for the Internet at a time when digital camera resolutions were much lower and not suitable for high-quality printing. One of the big strengths of the Internet is that it allows you to create your own simple website, blog or photo showcase where you can post a few images along with as much or little text as you like. This is a good way to start out and you'll get valuable feedback on how you can improve both your models and what and how you write about them. My first printed article was for the very first issue of

AFV Modeller magazine of the UK. The editor, David Parker, had seen my work on the Internet and asked if I was interested in writing an article for the new magazine. At this time I was using a traditional film Goko macro camera but as soon as higher-resolution digital cameras became available at affordable prices I bought one. I then got in touch with a few other magazines, sending some sample images and from there I started writing articles for each model I built. It was also the internet that provided me with the opportunity to write my first Osprey book as the publishers had seem some of my work on the Missing Lynx model website. Ultimately, I'm not a professional photographer, model maker or writer. As long as you can do these things to a reasonable standard then publishing articles will be open to you.

Above: This shot has a higher f-stop of 8.0 and almost the entire model is sharp and in focus. This image was taken very close up and so pulling back a little and cropping down would be enough to fix the slight blur right at the back around the idler wheel.

Below: The first page of my first magazine article. This was in *AFV Modeller* magazine issue 1, published back in 2001. (Image copyright AFV Modeller Ltd.)

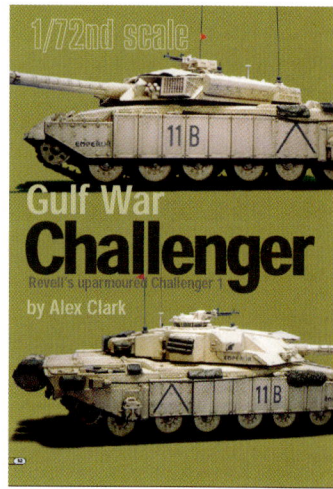

GALLERY

In this chapter I present a number of the models I've built over the last few years. Between them they illustrate all of the techniques I've described in this book and cover many different construction methods and paint finishes. Along with the all-important photos I've also included some additional information on the kits themselves; any aftermarket additions and accessories; scratch-built items and the finishing techniques and colours are described. Additional photos can be found on my website: http://www.small-scale-armour.co.uk.

SCHWERE WERMACHT SCHLEPPER WITH FLAK 43

I built this model using two separate Maco kits, one of the base halftrack and the other of the gun. Since then Maco have released the two kits in a single package. Maco are one of the newer and smaller injection-moulded kit manufacturers but the quality of their products is high. They make some of the less mainstream subjects that have largely been ignored by the larger manufacturers. I made some small improvements to the vehicle but spent most of the time improving the Flak gun. This involved rebuilding the detail on the gun itself and thinning the gun shield down. I also made a spent shell basket from a wire frame covered in etched mesh as this wasn't included in the kit. Maco now also sell a detail set that includes a basket. The pictures also show the additions I made to the base of the gun – these enable it to be secured to the vehicle cargo bed. I finished the model in a sprayed three-colour camouflage using Humbrol enamels. The figure is from a Dragon vehicle and figure combination set.

STURMTIGER

The Sturmtiger assault mortar was one of Dragon's earlier offerings in 1/72nd scale and features

a diecast upper hull with moulded-on tools. The detail of the diecast parts is somewhat soft but a resin replacement upper

hull from Atak, complete with pre-moulded *Zimmerit*, came to the rescue. I also replaced most of the lower hull with parts from the Revell late Tiger I kit due to its superior detail. This included the soft vinyl track that was swapped for Revell's hard plastic link and length versions. Being quite a plain-looking vehicle I left the engine compartment opened up and added a resin engine from Extratech. I made a number of other improvements to the kit using a few photo-etched parts and some scratch-built items, notably the ammo lifting crane. I painted it in a generic soft-edged camouflage using Humbrol enamels.

SDKFZ 9 FAMO

Revell's Famo is an excellent kit but benefited from the addition of details from the Trumpeter kit such as the engine and smaller lower chassis parts. The tarp is a resin item from MR Models and to allow the stowage in the cargo bed to be seen I cut the rear of this away and recreated a rolled-back portion using tissue paper soaked in dilute white PVA glue. I also added some photo-etched and homemade parts and filled the cargo bed with a variety of aftermarket stowage. It was painted in DAK colours using the hairspray technique with a base colour of Humbrol enamel and an application of Revell Afrikabraun (17) acrylic over the top.

PANZER IV AUSF. F

This is the excellent kit from Dragon to which I made some improvements to the smaller details. I also replaced the road wheels with the better ones from the Revell Nashorn kit and replaced the fenders with plastic strips and photo-etched tread plate. The resin tracks were given to me by another modeller who scratch-built and cast new ones himself. These feature hollow guide horns and even built-in track sag along the top run. I'm hoping he'll get the master parts for these commercially cast at some point. The model was finished with Humbrol enamel for the base grey colour and Revell acrylic white applied using the hairspray technique. The crew figures are AB white metal with resin heads from MIG Productions.

M977 HEMTT

I built the Academy M977 heavy truck as a vehicle serving in Iraq. Many of these vehicles had additional field-applied armour mostly consisting of metal plates around the cab area. The model was based on an all-green vehicle shown in the book *Armoured HEMTT* from Tankograd Publishing. This vehicle also had an MG ring fitted above the cab that I scratch-built from plastic strip and sheet. I improved and replaced many small details and used excellent resin wheels from Armory. These are of a later tread pattern and match the style of those fitted to the vehicle I was modelling. The stowage in the rear is a mix of homemade and aftermarket items. The model was painted using the pre-shading technique with Humbrol enamels.

StuG IV (mid version)

Prior to the release of the Dragon StuG IV kits, the only injection-moulded option was the poor offering from Revell. Previously I'd converted a Revell Panzer IV using parts from a StuG III to produce a late version StuG IV and this was featured in one of my earlier Osprey books. I was pleased to see the release of this kit as it is a vast improvement on the Revell one. I detailed it with a combination of photo-etched and homemade parts and replaced the overly thick *Schürzen* with plastic card versions (the kit includes

photo-etched ones but these are too narrow). The figures are also from Dragon and were taken from their

Panther + figures set. It was painted with Humbrol enamels with dry transfer markings from Archer.

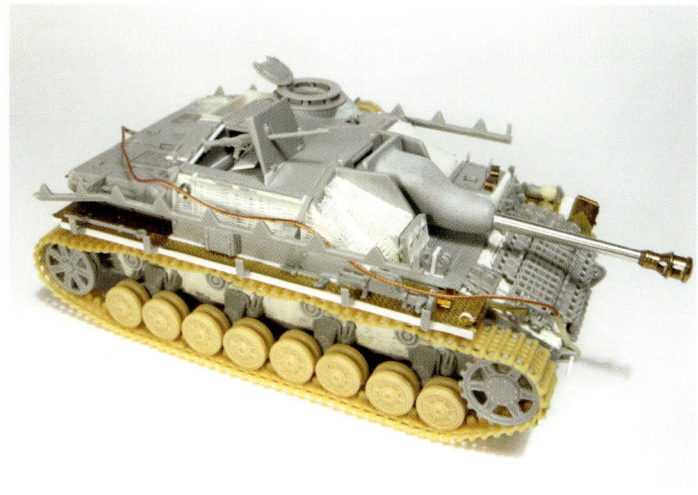

PANZER III AUSF. J (LATE)

Revell have two versions of the Panzer III in their range, the Ausf. L and Ausf. M. I'd wanted to build a DAK vehicle for some time so took the opportunity with this kit. Most of the DAK Panzer III vehicles were earlier versions with the short-barrelled gun. Some late Ausf. J variants featuring the longer-barrelled gun were also used by the DAK so I converted the Ausf. L kit to this version. It was quite a minor conversion involving mostly small detail changes. Tracks fitted at this time of the war featured hollow guide horns so I cut the solid ones off the link and length track and replaced them with hollow photo-etched ones cut from a Part photo-etched track set. This

was a bit fiddly but well worth the effort. I also used Part photo-etched detail sets for the fenders, allowing me to easily add realistic battle damage. For the crew I modified some MIG Productions DAK figures in order to get the

poses right, particularly for the figure sitting out of the turret side hatch. Painting was done with Humbrol enamels and Maskol to give a worn and weather-beaten finish. The markings are taken from the Archer dry transfer range.

JAGDTIGER (PORSCHE)

I modelled Dragon's Jagdtiger with Porsche suspension as a vehicle assigned to the Panzerjäger-Lehrgang in 1944. This was the third vehicle produced and was used as a training school vehicle. It was unusual in that it was fitted with tracks from an Elefant tank destroyer. I added a full, mostly scratch-built interior including the driver's, engine and main fighting compartment and until working on a scratch-built Grille II that was the most complex project I'd undertaken. I took the excellent link and length plastic tracks from Dragon's Elefant kit and detailed the exterior with photo-etched parts

from a Tiger II set. The model comes with a nicely executed *Zimmerit* finish but for this particular vehicle the *Zimmerit* didn't extend quite so far up the side of the vehicle. To fix this I sanded away

a strip at the top. The finish was achieved with Humbrol enamels and the weathering kept to a minimum as the vehicle didn't actually see action, or at least any action during the time frame I was modelling it in.

T-72B

There aren't many good post-war Russian vehicle models available so I was pleased to see Revell release a T-72M1. The kit is well done but represents an export version and suffers from an inaccurately shaped turret. After correcting this I decided to push on further and make a later up-armoured turret version seen on the 'B' model. I wanted to model a vehicle that saw service in Chechnya so I added explosive reactive armour bricks to the hull and turret as most photos show the vehicles with these fitted. To make the bricks I took some from the Revell T-80BV kit and reshaped them as they are too wide. To save repeating this step many times I cast resin copies. The crew are resin figures from the Armory range with the heads from a Dragon figure set. I painted it with Humbrol enamels using the pre-shading method and the markings are from a MIG Productions transfer set.

JAGDPANZER 38 'HETZER'

I'd built an old Esci Hetzer many years ago. Whilst it still holds up as a reasonable kit it has some dimensional issues compared to plans from the Panzertracts books. A few years back UM released a much better version, which is shown here. It still has a few errors that I addressed, most notably the wheel rim shape. To fix this I modified a kit wheel with parts from an Esci wheel and plastic tube slices for the tyres and cast some copies. I improved the track detail by thinning the links and adding track pin ends although the track width is still too narrow and not quite right

for a Hetzer. I painted it in a hard-edged three-tone pattern using Humbrol enamels and Blu-Tack for masking. The worn whitewash was

achieved with the hairspray method and Revell acrylic white. The figure is kit bashed from a couple of MIG Productions resin figures.

MERKAVA IV

Cromwell Models have a number of easy-assemble resin kits as part of the Combat72 range. These have a minimum of parts and so take very little time to build. In fact most of them are just provided as a turret, gun barrel a few smaller items like crew hatches and single-piece hull. The hulls include wheels and tracks moulded as part of them which considering the excellent detail of the kits is quite an achievement. On this Merkava IV I replaced the side skirts as the bolt detail is a little heavy and the area behind them is solid – although this is only noticeable from low angles I still wanted to improve it. I created the replacement skirt panels from plastic sheet and

embossed the rivet and bolt detail from the rear. I painted and weathered it using Humbrol enamels and to achieve the elusive

modern Israeli sand I mixed one part Olive Drab (155) to three parts Khaki Drab (72). The resin figure is from Goffy Models.

NASHORN

This was my second attempt at modelling a destroyed and burnt-out vehicle and was based on a side profile photo in the first book in the *Panzerwrecks* series. It represents a vehicle that served with the Panzerjäger-Abteilung 525 in Italy, 1944. The base kit is Dragon with some scratch-built details including those in the driver's compartment. The most complex part that I added myself was the transmission of which I cast resin copies. I had it fitted on a small, temporary scenic base but plan at some point to make a new one for it.

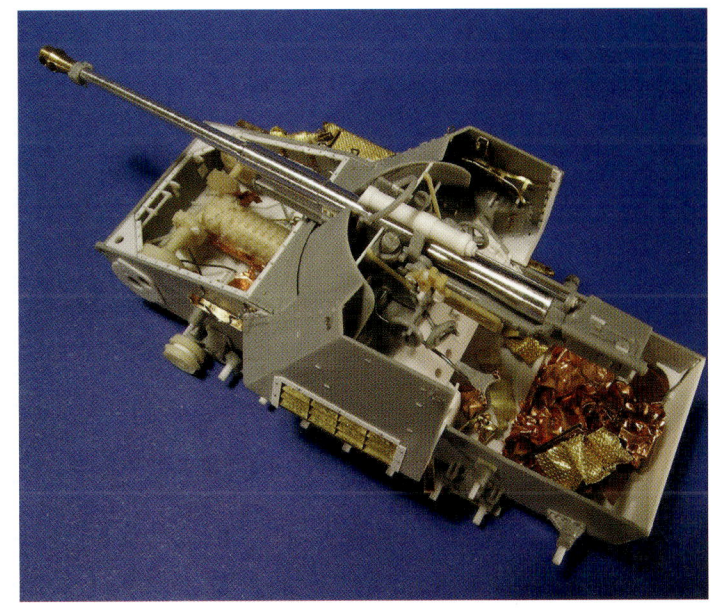

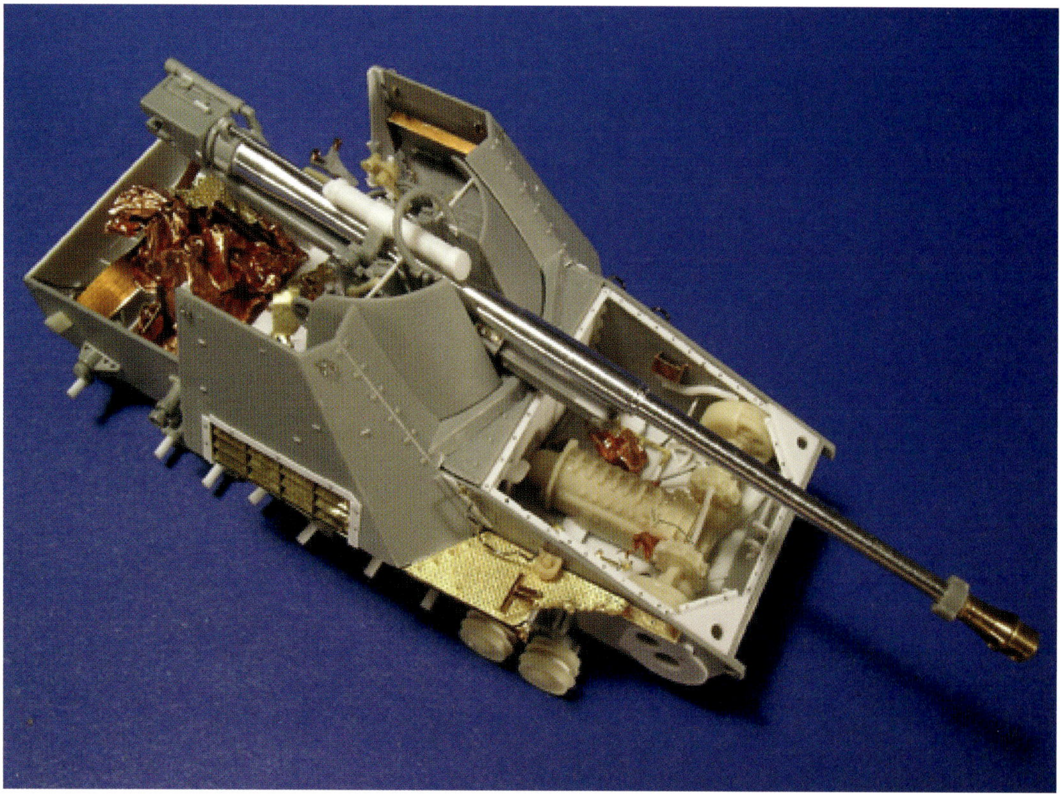

PANZER IV/70 (V)

This kit was the first that I added a scratch-built interior to. The base kit is from Hasegawa from which I took the lower hull tub and steel road wheels. I used the better detailed wheels from a Revell Panzer IV kit and rebuilt the upper hull from plastic sheet to achieve a more accurate scale thickness. I incorporated an Extratech resin transmission but scratch-built the engine block and fighting compartment interior. The roof is left as a separate part allowing it to be displayed as fitted or removed. Painting, weathering and finishing were done with Humbrol enamels and Archer transfers.

STURMPANZER IV 'BRUMMBAR' (LATE)

I built this late version Sturmpanzer IV before one was released by Trumpeter. The base kit is Revell's late Panzer IV Ausf. H with a replacement upper hull from AlBy. This resin conversion is actually intended for the overly long Esci Panzer IV model so I cut off the resin glacis and engine deck that was based on the Esci versions to just leave the central casemate. Many photos of late versions show steel wheels fitted at each station and an application of *Zimmerit*. I found an interesting camouflage pattern on a vehicle without *Zimmerit* and with steel wheels only fitted at the front that I wanted to replicate. For this I used Humbrol enamels with masking done using Blu-Tack. Markings are from the ever-reliable Archer dry transfer range.

PANZER IV AUSF. H

This is Revell's kit modelled as a burnt-out vehicle. The engine compartment and some of the driving compartment details are from Extratech. The turret and fighting compartment interiors are scratch-built. The fenders and some of the smaller details are photo-etched items from Part.

THE WORKBENCH

Along with the scratch-built Grille 17, I've got a number of part-finished projects on the go at various stages of completion. Like many modellers I tend to sometimes stop work on an existing model in order to start something fresh and new. I invariably return to these and try my best to get them finished.

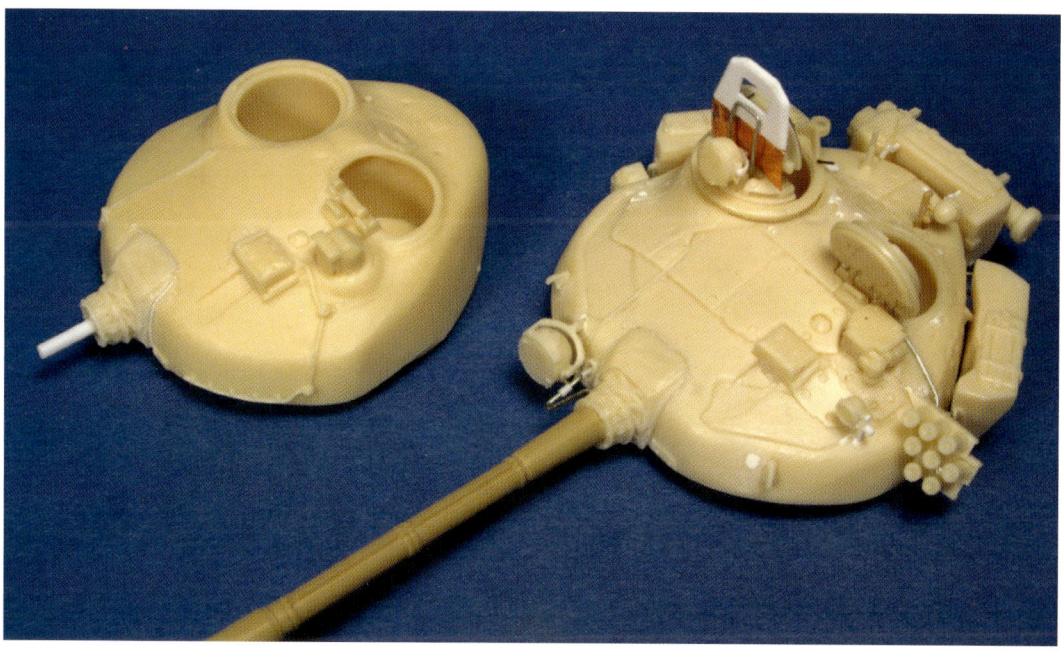

I'm working on several T-72 variants to go with the T-72B described earlier. Shown here are turrets for an A / M1 version along with the uparmoured B turret.

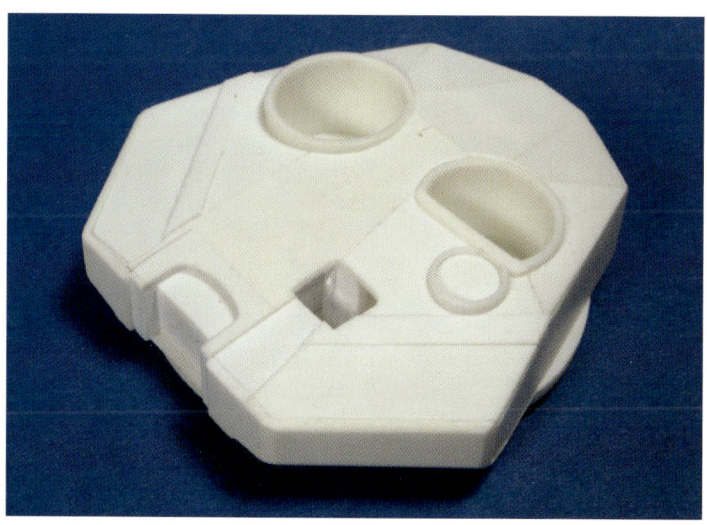

The T-90 is the latest incarnation of the T-72 family. This is a scratch-built welded turret seen on later versions such as the T-90A and T-90SA.

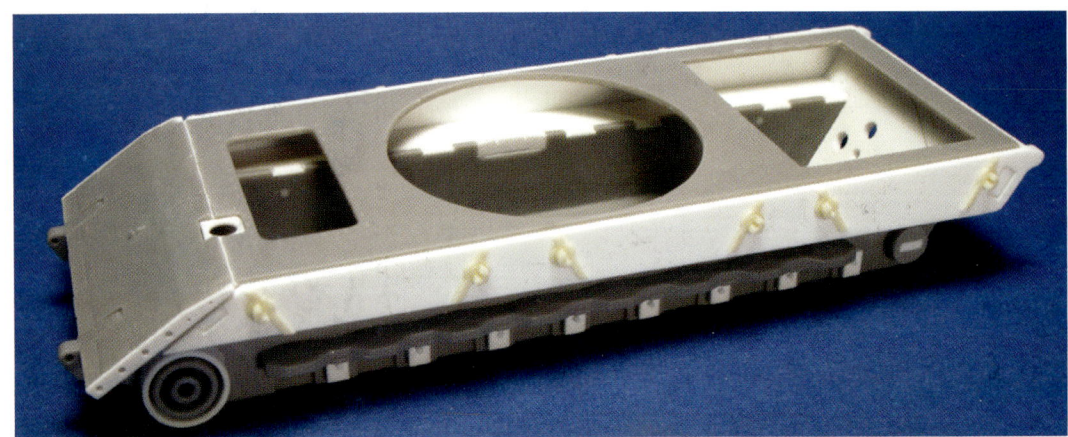

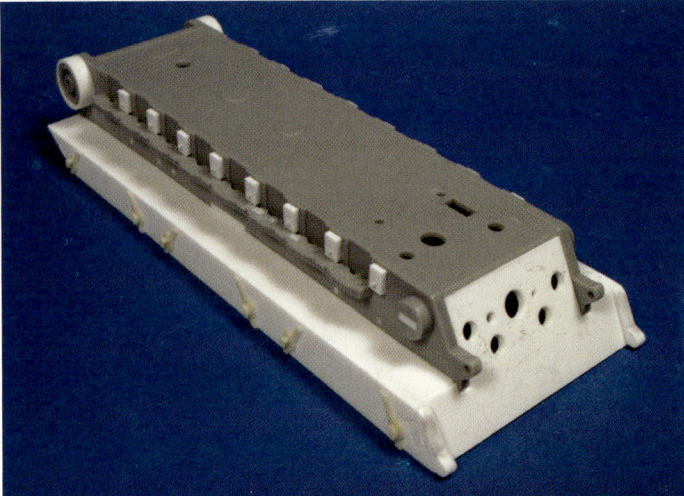

Dragon's E-100 super heavy tank is lacking in detail in some areas and is inaccurate in others. I'm building this as the prototype found as a largely complete hull at the end of the war.

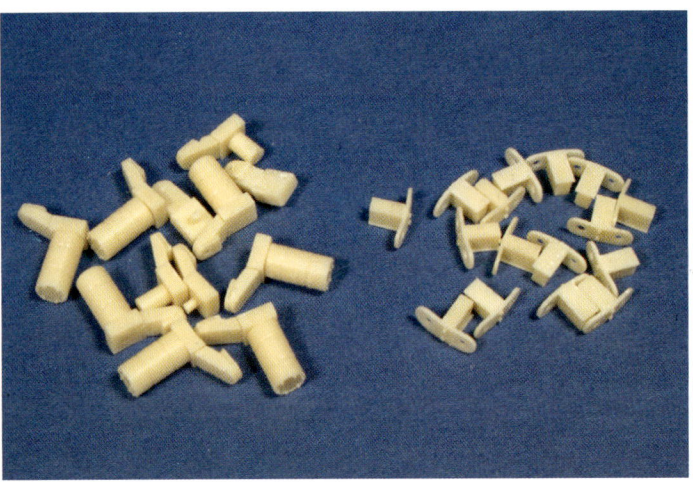

I'm modelling the hull as shown on several photographs with most of the roadwheels missing. For this I've cast copies of the suspension arms minus the wheels themselves.

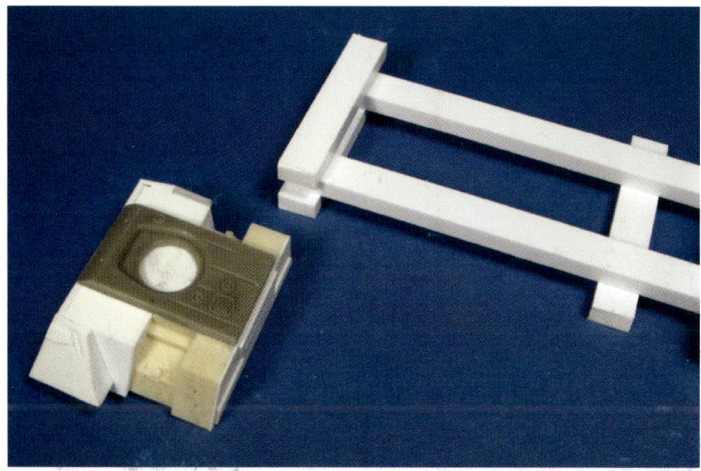

This is the very early progress of a scratch-built Russian BTR-80 armoured car. There is a kit from Trumpeter that is inaccurate in both details and dimensions so I decided to have a go making one myself. As I plan a few variants I've broken it down into small sub-assemblies to make it easier to cast copies.

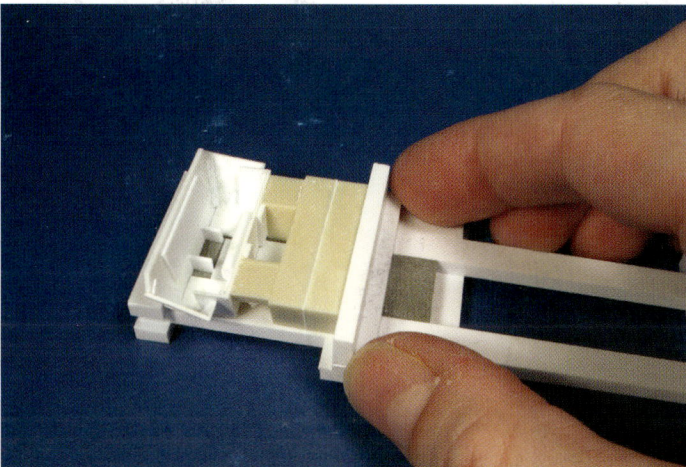

I made a small support jig to help ensure the parts all line up straight and true as I assemble them.

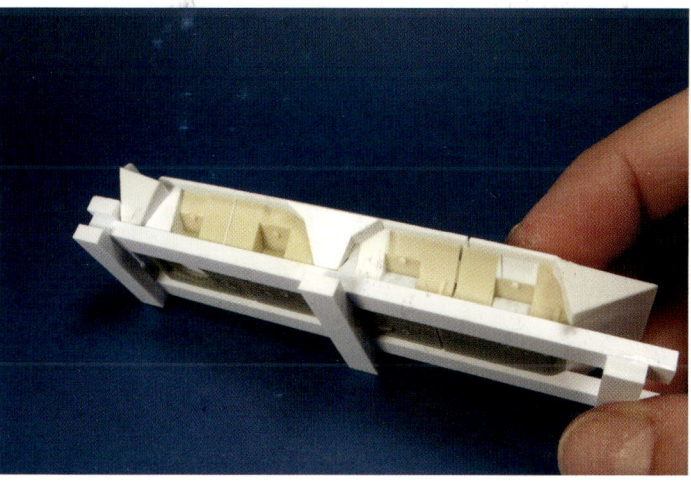

The four sub-sections of the lower hull are shown lined up on the jig. A few more details need to be added, and then I'll look to casting some resin copies.

FURTHER READING AND REFERENCES

There are many resources available to help you improve your modelling skills and I'll take a look at some of them here. Some of these are specifically aimed at small-scale modellers whilst others cover a range of scales but have a sizeable small-scale content. I've also included a list of sources and suppliers for some of the tools, accessories and books I use the most often.

MAGAZINES

Magazines are one of the most readily available resources and there are now a huge number of them covering many different languages. In the past it would have been difficult to purchase many of these due to them being published in other countries but the Internet and online ordering has made them much more accessible. Many locally published magazines will be available at hobby shops and newsagents, and model shows are a good source of magazines – especially if you're looking to purchase back issues. Most of these magazines contain some small-scale articles to varying degrees. Many also feature articles on real vehicles, with photo walk-arounds, technical details and histories that will be of interest to modellers of any scale. I find the articles on builds in other scales of interest too as they describe interesting techniques or finishes that can be applied to smaller scale models. There is one magazine in particular that is worthy of mention here and that

Minitracks magazine is a bilingual publication from France that is completely devoted to small-scale modelling. (Image copyright Editions du Barbotin)

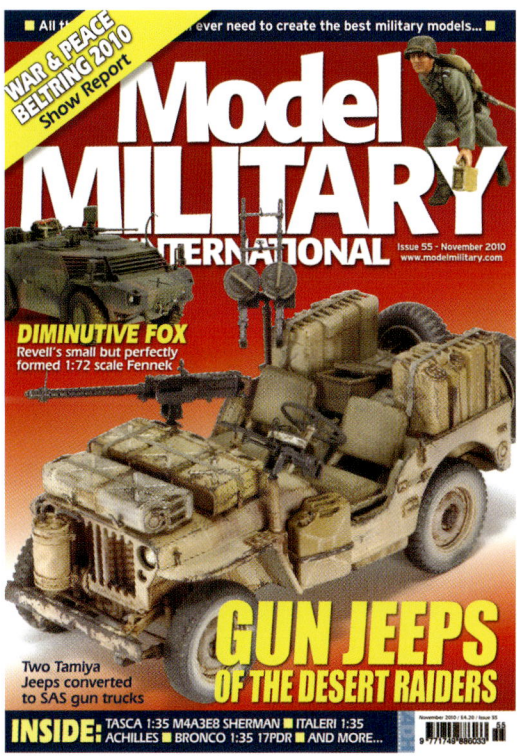

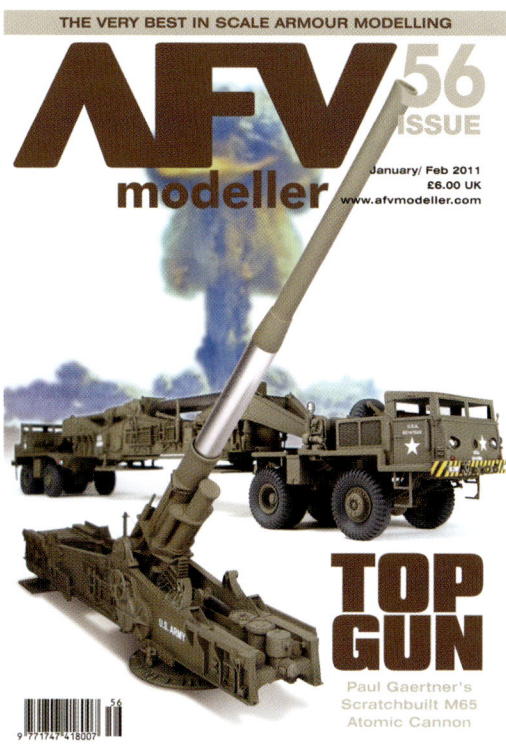

Some magazines now offer electronic downloads to allow them to be viewed on PCs and other electronic devices.

(Images copyright ADH Publishing and AFV modeller Ltd. respectively)

is *Minitracks*. This is a French publication and is unusual in that it is solely devoted to small-scale modelling. It's also bilingual (in French and English) which will broaden its appeal and market. It's been established for quite a number of years now and although it's undergone a few transformations in design and publication frequency during this time, it's always maintained a very high quality of modelling articles.

In the UK there are a number of magazines covering multiple scales and several have shown a gradual increase in the number of small-scale topics. *Military in Scale* is a monthly publication that also covers aircraft but the AFV content is very good indeed. *AFV Modeller* is published bimonthly and features in-depth articles with excellent photography. *Military Modelcraft International* has featured quite a number of impressive

small-scale articles and has a section devoted to small-scale news and reviews. *Military Modelling* covers figures too but also has some excellent technical and historical articles. It has a long-running feature, 'Small Scale Scene', which has good small-scale content regarding news of new releases. Two other magazines are *Tamiya Magazine* and *Model Military International*, both from the same publisher. These also cover articles in many scales but *Model Military International* is purely vehicle based whilst *Tamiya Magazine* covers all sort of other topics such as aircraft, cars, ships and so on. There has also been a move to sell electronic copies of magazines. *AFV Modeller* can be bought as both traditional paper copies or as electronic pdf files (Portable Document Format) and these can be read on PCs, smart phones and other electronic devices. In fact individual articles can be purchased allowing a reader to choose only those of particular interest. The publishers of *Tamiya Model Magazine* and *Model Military International* have entered the electronic market with both magazines being available for Apple devices such as the iPhone and iPad tablet. I suspect this is something that other magazines will also follow suit on.

Moving overseas, I own at least of few issues of some of the major magazines from several other countries. *Steelmasters* is a glossy French magazine that regularly features small-scale articles. Although all in French, the large step-by-step photos make it very easy to follow. One of the high-quality Italian magazines is *Steel Art* and as with *Steelmasters*, it has very good articles with large, clear photos. From Spain the magazine *Xtreme Modelling* is of similar quality and is printed in both Spanish and English language editions. I haven't seen a recent issue of the Japanese magazine

Armour Modelling but those I do own contain some very impressive models and in particular dioramas. A little later, in the Sources section, I give a list of contact details for all of these magazines.

BOOKS

I couldn't fail to mention the Osprey series here of course, notably the Osprey Modelling series of books. I authored two of the books in this series, both covering 1/72nd-scale modelling. These are *Modelling*

There are many books that have some small-scale content but not as many that only deal with 1/72nd scale. Two previous books I wrote for the Osprey Modelling series cover Panzer IV and Tiger variants. The book *Diorama Addicted* by Justo Mira describes many techniques for building small-scale dioramas and is illustrated with some fantastic examples. There are a couple of scale plan books aimed purely at 1/72 scale. These are both by George Bradford and cover Axis (shown here) and Allied vehicles of World War II respectively.

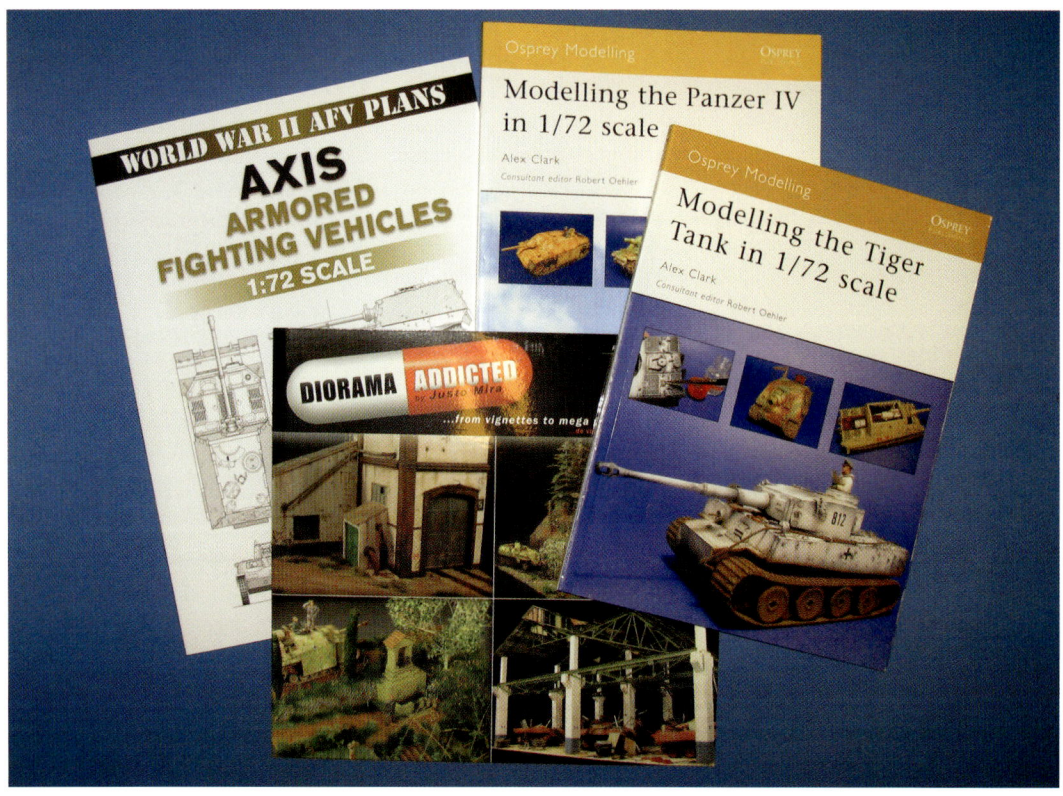

the Panzer IV in 1/72 scale (no. 17) and *Modelling the Tiger Tank in 1/72 scale* (no. 18). A number of the other titles in this series also cover single subjects or families and have some small-scale content. There aren't many other small-scale-only books that I'm aware of that are currently in print. One excellent publication is *Diorama Addicted* from the Spanish company AK-Interactive. This is written by in my opinion one of the very best small-scale diorama builders, Justo Mira, and features detailed coverage of many techniques for building small-scale dioramas.

A book dedicated to Airfix 1/76th-scale models is *Build and Convert Airfix Military Models* by Tom Cole. This book hasn't been published at the time of writing this but is due out at about the same time as this book.

Moving on to non-modelling books, there are many publishers of books dealing with real vehicles. From a modelling perspective the most useful are those that contain detail photographs and walk-around features. Scale plans are another extremely useful addition and

whilst sometimes these are to 1/72nd scale they are often larger. In these cases they can be resized on a photocopying machine.

MUSEUMS

I'm not going to try and give an exhaustive list of armoured vehicle museums around the world. Most modellers will know of any major ones in the country they live in or can easily find them with a quick Internet search. I've been to a few over the years, and at Duxford in the UK I gained permission for a private viewing of the post-war Russian vehicle collection. The collections rotated and this one wasn't currently being displayed at the time. Instead it was being stored outside out of main view. I rang ahead to speak to the

Armoured vehicle museums sometimes rotate their displays so if there's anything you're particularly interested in viewing it's worth ringing ahead to check. If you explain you're an enthusiast you may even get the chance to get closer to the vehicles than usual.

person in charge and explained my great interest in their collection and that I was planning a visit. This was met with a very helpful and positive response and when I arrived not only was I able to take all the photos I wanted, but I was given freedom to climb both on and into the vehicles. This was a great opportunity to get good close-up shots and to take measurements of the vehicles. Some museums don't allow photography by the general public so it's always worth contacting them before a planned visit to check their rules. They will sometimes give special permission to take photos and maybe even to get closer to the vehicles than would normally be possible, especially if they know you are an enthusiast. Something to be aware of regarding historical vehicles is that museums and collections may have restored them to a more pristine condition than when originally found. Doing so might have involved using modern parts or modern remakes of the originals. Truly preserved vehicles will be untouched in this regard but in many cases these will have damaged or missing fittings. In any case I try to cross reference with plans and period photographs to double check this.

THE INTERNET

There is an ever increasing number of model- and armour-related websites on the Internet and I've been following some of the longest-standing ones since the mid-1990s. One of the biggest strengths of the Internet is the sheer volume of information and expertise that is available. This comes at a cost, however, and sometimes it can be hard to find what you are looking for. There is also a lot of inaccurate information and opinions out there to be aware of. The most useful aspects of the Internet from my own experience are that it gives you the ability to find out answers to what can be quite specific and specialized technical questions – with the caveats listed above of course. The other use is on the purely modelling side and many sites have forums where modellers display their in-progress work. There are many examples of

stunning work from around the world regularly posted on these, keeping the content fresh and inspiring. Being able to learn from these and even ask the modellers behind them questions on techniques etc. is a valuable opportunity. Posting your own work is just as enlightening although some critics can be harsh so be prepared for honest opinions! The sites listed below are some of the larger, longer-standing ones that I frequent regularly:

www.missing-lynx.com

www.armorama.com

www.track-link.net

There are also some excellent small-scale-only sites. Again there are too many to list and I have a comprehensive list of these on my website at:

www.small-scale-armour.co.uk

SOURCES

Throughout the earlier chapters I've referred to various manufacturers of the tools, paints and accessories I use most often. I've presented a list here of contact details of either the original source or of agents and distributors that they can be obtained from. They are all open to international orders/enquiries or would be able to point you to a local source. For more standard items such as widely available kits or paints from the major manufacturers I haven't listed any details. I would imagine most if not all readers would be able to source these themselves. Similarly I haven't listed every online hobby shop I use or have used as they are just too numerous. One I will mention however is Tracks and Troops. This shop is based in the Czech Republic and is completely dedicated to small-scale military kits, accessories and tools. They also fulfil overseas orders.

http://www.tracks-n-troops.eu/shop/

milan.vins@tracks-n-troops.eu

E. Kostala 1006

530 12 Pardubice

Czech Republic

CONSTRUCTION MATERIALS AND TOOLS

JLC Razor Saw:
Available from http://www.rollmodels.com/ and
http://www.tracks-n-troops.eu/shop/

Plastic sheet, strip, rod and tubing:
Evergreen Scale Models
http://www.evergreenscalemodels.com/

The Nutter – rivet-making tool:
The Small Shop – aka Kalama Precision Machine
http://www.thesmallshop.com
smallshop@thesmallshop.com
PO Box 580
Kalama
WA 98625
USA

Resin casting materials and equipment:
Sylmasta
http://www.sylmasta.com/
sales@sylmasta.com
Unit 1 Dales Yard
Lewes Road
Scaynes Hill
West Sussex
RH17 7PG
UK

Copper tow cables:
Eureka XXL
http://www.eurekaxxl.com/
eureka-xxl@wp.pl

PAINTING AND FINISHING PRODUCTS

Dry transfers and markings:
Archer Fine Transfers
http://www.archertransfers.com/
info@archertransfers.com
PO Box 1277
Youngsville

NC 27596
USA

Marking stencils:
Scale Link
http://www.scalelink.co.uk
info@scalelink.co.uk
Farrington
Dorset
DT11 8RA
UK

PRESENTATION PRODUCTS

Wooden display bases:
Wiremill Designs
http://www.woodenbases.co.uk/
wiremill@btinternet.com
Four Crosses, Wiremill Lane
Lingfield
Surrey
RH7 6HJ
UK

Nameplates and plaques:
Name It!
http://www.nameitplates.co.uk/
Nameit@fsmail.net
12 Savay Lane, Denham Green
Denham
Buckinghamshire
UB9 5NH
UK

MAGAZINES

AFV Modeller
www.afvmodeller.com
david@afvmodeller.com
176 Newbridge Street
Newcastle upon Tyne
NE1 2TE
UK

Military in Scale
http://www.militaryinscale.com/
hello@traplet.com
Traplet Publications Ltd
Traplet House
Pendragon Close
Malvern
Worcestershire
WR14 1GA
UK

Military Modelcraft International
http://mmi.guidelinepublications.co.uk/
Guideline Publications
Unit 3, Enigma Building
Bilton Road
Denbigh East
Bletchley
Buckinghamshire
MK1 1HW
UK

Military Modelling
http://www.militarymodelling.com/
Myhobbystore Ltd
Tower House
Sovereign Park
Market Harborough
Leicestershire
LE16 9EF
UK

Minitracks
http://www.minitracks.fr/
info@edbarbotin.com
Editions Du Barbotin
20, La Deniserie
28240 Les Corvees-les-Yys
France

Model Military International
http://www.modelmilitary.com/
editor@modelmilitary.com
ADH Publishing Ltd.
Doolittle Mill
Doolittle Lane
Totternhoe,
Bedfordshire
LU6 1QX
UK

Steel Art
http://www.aurigapublishing.it/
info@aurigapublishing.it
Auriga Publishing International Ltd.
Via Bressanone 17/1
16154 Genova
Italy

Steelmasters
http://steelmasters.histoireetcollections.com/en
Histoire et Collections
5 Avenue de la République
75541 Paris cedex 11
France

Tamiya Magazine
http://www.tamiyamodelmagazine.com/
modmagint@aol.com
ADH Publishing Ltd.
Doolittle Mill
Doolittle Lane
Totternhoe
Bedfordshire
LU6 1QX
UK

Xtreme Modelling
http://www.xtrememodelling.com/
info@xtrememodelling.com

INDEX

References to illustrations are shown in **bold**